SQL Built-In Functions and
Stored Procedures

SQL Built-In Functions and Stored Procedures

Mike Faust

MC PRESS

SQL Built-in Functions and Stored Procedures
Mike Faust

First Edition

First Printing—April 2005
Second Printing—May 2007

Every attempt has been made to provide correct information. However, the publisher and the author do not guarantee the accuracy of the book and do not assume responsibility for information included in or omitted from it.

The following terms are trademarks of International Business Machines Corporation in the United States, other countries, or both: IBM, AS/400, OS/400, and i5/OS. All other product names are trademarked or copyrighted by their respective manufacturers.

MC Press offers excellent discounts on this book when ordered in quantity for bulk purchases or special sales, which may include custom covers and content particular to your business, training goals, marketing focus, and branding interest.

For information regarding permissions or special orders, please contact:
MC Press
Corporate Offices
125 N. Woodland Trail
Lewisville, TX 75077 USA

For information regarding sales and/or customer service, please contact:
MC Press
P.O. Box 4300
Big Sandy, TX 75755-4300 USA

ISBN: 1-58347-054-9

Contents

Introduction

Like its predecessors—the System/36, System/38, and AS/400—the IBM eServer iSeries is one of the most reliable computer systems available. When you add to that reliability the number of development languages available, you have what is arguably the best platform for mission-critical business applications. When it comes to accessing a relational database like DB2, Structured Query Language (SQL) is the de facto standard language of choice. The iSeries DB2 implementation is no exception. SQL does have its shortcomings, but we can work around these shortcomings through the use of user-defined functions and stored procedures.

In this book, we'll examine what user-defined functions and stored procedures are, how to create them, and how to use them within applications. At the same time, we'll examine a set of truly useful user-defined functions and stored procedures, which have been included with this book. Once you've completed this book, you'll not only have a new toolset of useful functions and procedures, you'll also have the tools to create more of your own.

We'll start out by exploring the iSeries flavor of SQL. We'll cover the software requirements and prerequisites. We'll also take a look at some basic SQL statements and examine the general syntax used in SQL. In addition to this, we'll examine how we would use each of these to perform specific database tasks on the iSeries. This should give you the basic SQL skills required to complete the rest of the book.

Next, we'll delve into the world of the built-in functions and stored procedures within DB2 for the iSeries implementation of SQL. We'll explore what functions and stored procedures are and explain the difference between the two. We'll also take a look at the commonly used functions and stored procedures on the iSeries and explain how each of them would be used within an application.

Our next step will be to cover creating our own stored procedures. We'll explain what the different types of stored procedures available are and how to create each. Once we've explained how to create a stored procedure, we'll explore a special set of stored procedures included with this book and examine how to use each.

After that, we'll examine user-defined functions. Again, we'll cover the different types of user-defined functions available. As with the stored procedures, we'll also review the set of user-defined functions included with the book and examine how each one would be used from within an application.

Finally, we'll cover how to make full use of functions and stored procedures from within "non-SQL" languages. We'll also explore how to create SQL "batches"—that is, processes—that contain multiple SQL statements, which are executed like an old DOS batch file. Once you've completed this book, you'll be ready to take full advantage of SQL functions and stored procedures with your iSeries.

1

SQL on the iSeries

Structured Query Language (SQL) is the industry standard language for database access. While the American National Standards Institute (ANSI) has a defined SQL standard, within that standard, each relational database platform has its own unique "flavor" of SQL. This can include things as simple as command syntax and as complex as supported functions. In this chapter, we'll explore what makes the iSeries implementation of SQL unique. This chapter acts as an introduction to the SQL functionality on the iSeries. If you're already somewhat familiar with that functionality, you may want to skip ahead to chapter 2.

Software Requirements

To use the examples in this book, you'll need to have the DB2 Query Manager and SQL Development Toolkit licensed program installed on your iSeries. This licensed program gives you a handful of useful tools, including the Query Manager report writing tool as well as the precompilers, which allow you to embed SQL code within other programming languages (SQL RPG, for example).

This licensed program also gives you the STRSQL interactive SQL command line utility. This utility comes in handy if you need to run ad hoc queries (i.e., action queries to modify records in a database on the fly). Throughout this book, many of the examples we cover will be executed from within this utility. Later in the book, we'll also be exploring the use of functions and procedures from client applications developed in Microsoft Access, Visual Basic (VB), and Active Server Pages (ASP).

SQL Tools

Throughout this book, we'll use several utilities (both GUI and green-screen) that make it easier to work with SQL statements on the iSeries. The STRSQL command can be executed from an iSeries command line. This command starts the interactive SQL utility. When you enter this utility, press the F4 key to display a list of the available SQL commands that can be executed from within the interactive SQL session. When a SELECT statement is entered, the resulting data can be either displayed to the screen or sent to a printer or output file. This selection is made by pressing F13 from within STRSQL to display the Interactive SQL Session Services menu and selecting option 1 for Current Session Attributes. Figure 1.1 shows the screen that is displayed.

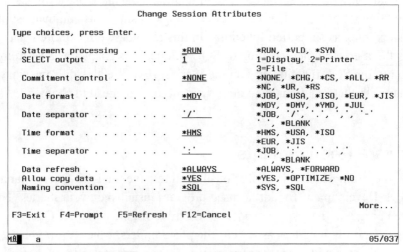

Figure 1.1: SQL SELECT output can be redirected from this screen.

This screen shows that option 1 has been selected for the "SELECT output" field. If you select option 2, you'll be prompted for the printer name. If you select option 3, you'll be presented with parameters for the file and library to contain the output data. Notice that you can specify other options here as well, such as the data and time format and the naming convention.

iSeries Navigator also includes an SQL tool. You can access this utility by first expanding the Databases option and clicking on your system name and then selecting Run an SQL Script link from the right side of the lower pane in iSeries Navigator. The window shown in Figure 1.2 will be displayed.

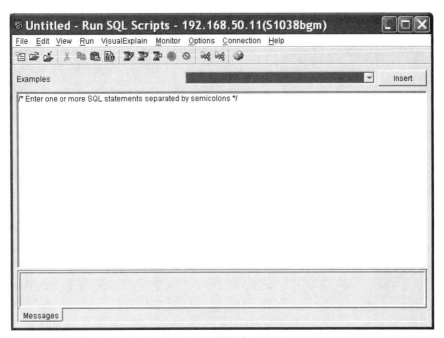

Figure 1.2: iSeries Navigator includes an SQL Script tool.

You can use this screen in much the same way that you'd use STRSQL. The Examples drop-down list contains templates of SQL statements to perform common tasks. Later, we'll examine using this application to create functions and procedures. As we examine sample SQL statements throughout this book, either of these two tools can be used.

Exploring SQL Statements

Let's take a look at the components and functions of the various SQL statements.

Starting with the Basics

Probably the single most common individual SQL statement is the SELECT statement, which allows you to define a set of data to be retrieved from a database. Figure 1.3 shows the basic structure of a SELECT statement.

```
SELECT field_list
FROM table_definition(s)
WHERE condition_expression
GROUP BY group_field_list
ORDER BY sort_field_list
HAVING group_level_conditions
```

Figure 1.3: This is the basic structure of an SQL SELECT statement.

Within this example, the FROM clause is required. However, the other clauses shown are optional. The field_list value would be replaced by a comma-delimited list of fields or simply an asterisk to return all fields from the defined table(s). The table_definition value can be a list of joined tables, along with a definition of how they are to be joined, or simply a physical or logical file name. (We'll examine joining tables a little later on.) The condition_expression on the WHERE clause determines exactly which records will be returned from the defined table or tables. The group_field_list used with the GROUP BY clause indicates that the data set returned is to be summarized by the list of fields provided. When a GROUP BY clause is specified, all of the column names appearing in the field_list either must appear in the group_field_list or must be a column function (SUM, AVG, MIN, MAX, etc.). The sort_field_list defined on the ORDER BY clause defines the sort order for the result set. The group_level_conditions defined on the HAVING clause is used in much the same way that the WHERE clause is used except that the condition defined here is checked only after a GROUP BY is processed. This allows you to use a column function as part of a condition.

4

As you can see, the SELECT statement can take on many forms. The code below shows a very simple form of a SELECT statement.

```
SELECT *
FROM QSYS2.SYSTABLES
```

This example uses the SQL naming convention in place of the SYS file naming convention, which would use the format library/file. This statement would return all columns (or fields) from the file SYSTABLES in library QSYS2. A slightly more complex version of this statement could be used to select only required fields under specified conditions, as shown below:

```
SELECT TABLE_NAME, TABLE_TYPE
FROM QSYS2.SYSTABLES
WHERE TABLE_SCHEMA = 'QSYS'
ORDER BY TABLE_NAME
```

This example would display only the columns TABLE_NAME and TABLE_TYPE for records with a TABLE_SCHEMA value of 'QSYS'. The result set would be sorted by the TABLE_NAME column. To further elaborate on this example, we can add grouping clauses to create a summary result set, as shown below:

```
SELECT TABLE_SCHEMA, COUNT(*) AS TABLE_COUNT, SUM(ROW_LENGTH) AS
TOTAL_ROW_LEN
FROM QSYS2.SYSTABLES
WHERE TABLE_TYPE = 'P'
GROUP BY TABLE_SCHEMA
HAVING COUNT(*)>10
```

This example would display library names (TABLE_SCHEMA) and the number of physical files within each library, along with the total length of rows between all tables within the library. The HAVING clause is used to include only libraries containing more than 10 physical files.

A slight variation of the SELECT statement can be found in SELECT INTO. This statement is used to pass values from a defined SELECT statement into host variables in a stored procedure or embedded SQL within an RPG program.

When using SELECT INTO, no more than one row can be returned at a time. This means that your statement must return results containing unique results.

While the SELECT statement is used to retrieve data from a database, other statements are used to manipulate a database. The DELETE statement, as its name would suggest, is used to remove rows from a table. Figure 1.4 shows the syntax used with the DELETE statement.

```
DELETE
FROM table_definition(s)
WHERE condition_expression
```

Figure 1.4: The DELETE statement is used to remove records from a table.

This statement takes on a somewhat simpler form than the SELECT statement, but the FROM and WHERE clauses function exactly as they do with the SELECT statement. Below is a sample DELETE statement.

```
DELETE FROM MYLIB.MYFILE WHERE RCSTAT = 'D'
```

This statement shows the code that would be used to remove all records from the table MYFILE where the field RCSTAT is equal to 'D'.

The UPDATE statement takes on a similar structure to the DELETE statement. Figure 1.5 shows what this structure looks like.

```
UPDATE table_definition(s)
SET field = value
WHERE condition_expression
```

Figure 1.5: The UPDATE statement is used to modify data within a database.

You'll notice that we don't precede the table_definition value with the FROM clause here. The SET clause is used to define the field to be modified and the value to place in that field. As it does in the SELECT and DELETE statements, the WHERE clause filters which records will be affected.

The INSERT INTO statement adds new records to a table. Figure 1.6 shows the syntax used with this statement.

```
INSERT INTO table_definition(s) (field list)
VALUES (value list)

Or

INSERT INTO table_definition(s) (field list)
Select statement
```

Figure 1.6: The INSERT INTO statement accepts these two possible formats.

The table_definition value identifies the table into which the records will be inserted. This value can optionally be followed by a list of fields to be populated. If this list is not supplied, it is assumed that values will be provided for all fields within the destination table. The values to be inserted can by supplied using one of two methods:

1. A VALUES list, containing the specific values to be inserted into a single row

2. A SELECT statement that will return one or more rows to be inserted into the table

The number of values specified must match the number of fields to be inserted into. This is true for both the VALUES clause and the SELECT statement option.

Slightly More Complex

Each statement examined here becomes somewhat more complicated when you take multiple files into consideration. The method used for retrieving data from multiple tables is different for each of the statements we've examined so far.

The SELECT statement uses the JOIN clause to define multiple tables as its data source. The JOIN clause has several modifiers that define the type of join to be used. Table 1.1 below breaks down each of these options and describes how each one is used.

Table 1.1: JOIN Clauses and Their Descriptions

Join Type	Description
INNER JOIN/JOIN	This join includes only rows where records are matched from both tables specified.
LEFT JOIN/LEFT OUTER JOIN	This join includes all rows from the table specified on the left side of the join expression and matched rows from the table specified on the right side.
RIGHT JOIN/RIGHT OUTER JOIN	This join includes all rows from the table specified on the right side of the join expression and matched rows from the table specified on the left side.
LEFT EXCEPTION JOIN/EXCEPTION JOIN	When this join is used, data is returned for records from the table on the left side of the join that has no matching records for the table on the right side. Field values from the table on the right side of the join will be returned as *null*.
RIGHT EXCEPTION JOIN	This join returns data from the table specified on the right side of the join expression where no matching records are found for the table on the left side. Field values from the table on the left side of the join will be returned as *null*.
CROSS JOIN	This join combines each row from the table specified on the left side of the expression with each row from the table specified on the right side of the expression.

Which of these joins you use depends on what your intentions are. An INNER JOIN would be used in circumstances where you know that matched records will exist in the tables in both sides of the join or where you want to see only the matched records. This means that if the table on the left side of the expression does not find a matching value in the table on the right side, the record will be omitted. This also means that if a value exists in the table on the right side and doesn't have a matching value in the table on the left, the record will also be omitted. A good example of how this is used would be an order header file with line detail records. Figure 1.7 shows an example of this type of statement.

```
SELECT *
FROM MYLIB.ORDHEADR INNER JOIN  MYLIB.ORDDETL
    ON ORDHEADR.ORDNO = ORDDETL.ORDNO
```

Figure 1.7: This is a sample of using the INNER JOIN operator.

8

This example would return all fields from ORDHEADR and all fields from ORDDETL where the field ORDNO is matched between the two tables.

Table 1.2 shows a graphic example of how the two tables would combine into the resulting data set.

Table 1.2: Example of INNER JOIN

ORDHEADR

ORDNO	CUSNO	ORDAT	ORVAL
12345	ABC	20050101	500.00
12346	DEF	20050115	350.00
12347	GHI	20050110	160.00
12348	AAA	20041231	0.00

ORDDETL

ORDNO	ORDLN	ORITM	ORQTY
12345	1	11111	5
12345	2	22222	10
12345	3	33333	16
12346	1	344A	5
12346	2	224B	10
12347	1	122DF	25
12347	2	11111	12

SELECT Statement Results

ORDNO	CUSNO	ORDAT	ORVAL	ORDNO	ORDLN	ORITM	ORQTY
12345	ABC	20050101	500.00	12345	1	11111	5
12345	ABC	20050101	500.00	12345	2	22222	10
12345	ABC	20050101	500.00	12345	3	33333	16
12346	DEF	20050115	350.00	12346	1	344A	5
12346	DEF	20050115	350.00	12346	2	224B	10
12347	GHI	20050110	160.00	12347	1	122DF	25
12347	GHI	20050110	160.00	12347	2	11111	12

As you can see in this example, when the tables are combined, the field values from ORDHEADR are repeated when multiple matching values exist in ORDDETL. You'll also notice that the row in ORDHEADR where ORDNO is 12348 does not have any matching values in ORDDETL; the row is omitted from the result set.

A left join includes all of the records from the table specified on the left side of the join and any matched records from the right side. This means that even if a record in the table on the left side of the join doesn't have a matching record in the table on the right side, the record is still included. An example of a situation where this might be used would be to retrieve comment records to be matched to a header record. In this type of situation, the comment records may or may not exist. Figure 1.8 shows an example of this.

```
SELECT *
FROM MYLIB.ORDHEADR LEFT JOIN MYLIB.COMMENTS
    ON ORDHEADR.ORDNO = COMMENTS.ORDNO
```

Figure 1.8: This example shows how the LEFT JOIN expression might be used.

This example will include all rows from the ORDHEADR table as well as any matching records from the COMMENTS table. Table 1.3 below shows how this data is combined.

Table 1.3: Example of LEFT JOIN

ORDHEADR				COMMENTS	
ORDNO	CUSNO	ORDAT	ORVAL	ORDNO	TEXT
12345	ABC	20050101	500.00	12345	Ship to Bob
12346	DEF	20050115	350.00	12346	Next-day air
12347	GHI	20050110	160.00	12347	No foam peanuts
12348	AAA	20041231	0.00	12347	Use recycled packing

Table 1.3: Example of LEFT JOIN (continued)

SELECT Statement Results					
ORDNO	CUSNO	ORDAT	ORVAL	ORDNO	TEXT
12345	ABC	20050101	500.00	12345	Ship to Bob
12346	DEF	20050115	350.00	12346	Next-day air
12347	GHI	20050110	160.00	12347	No foam peanuts
12347	GHI	20050110	160.00	12347	Use recycled packing
12348	AAA	20041231	0.00		

As you can see in this example, any records in the table on the left side of the expression that do not have any matching records on the right side of the expression will still appear in the result set. However, the field values from the right side of the expression will be null. A right join works in an opposite fashion to a left join. Figure 1.9 shows an example of the same statement coded as a right join.

```
SELECT *
FROM MYLIB.COMMENTS RIGHT JOIN MYLIB.ORDHEDR
     ON ORDHEDR.ORDNO = COMMENTS.ORDNO
```

Figure 1.9: Here's the RIGHT JOIN expression in action.

The results returned by this expression will be identical to the results in Table 1.3, except that the field order will appear differently because the primary table is now on the right side of the expression.

The LEFT and RIGHT EXCEPTION JOIN expressions are used to find mismatched records between a primary table and a secondary table. Figure 1.10 shows an example of a SELECT statement using a LEFT EXCEPTION JOIN expression.

11

```
SELECT *
FROM CUSTOMERS C LEFT EXCEPTION JOIN SALES S
ON C.CUSNO = S.CUSNO
```

Figure 1.10: The LEFT EXCEPTION JOIN expression locates mismatched records.

This example will display any records in the CUSTOMERS table that do not have any matching records in the SALES table. Note the letter following each of the table names. This represents an alias for each table, which allows us to use a simpler name to refer to the table within the rest of our statement. This can be especially useful when executing statements between tables with many common field names.

The CROSS JOIN expression combines all records from one table with all of the records from another. Because of this, a cross join doesn't require that join fields be defined. Each time a record is read from the table on the left side of the expression, all of the records from the table on the right side of the expression are returned. Figure 1.11 shows how a CROSS JOIN expression is used.

```
SELECT *
FROM TABLE1 CROSS JOIN TABLE2
```

Figure 1.11: The CROSS JOIN expression combines all records from tables on both sides of the expression.

When this statement is executed, it can result in a large volume of data being returned. Table 1.4 shows an example of how this data is combined.

Table 1.4: Example of CROSS JOIN

TABLE 1			TABLE 2	
RECN1	VALUE1		RECN2	VALUE2
1	100.75		1	12.76
2	200.25		2	115.95
3	195.55			

Table 1.4: Example of CROSS JOIN (continued)

SELECT Statement Results			
RECN1	VALUE1	RECN2	VALUE2
1	100.75	1	12.76
1	100.75	2	115.95
2	200.25	1	12.76
2	200.25	2	115.95
3	195.55	1	12.76
3	195.55	2	115.95

As this example illustrates, the number of records returned by this statement would be equal to the number of records in the first table multiplied by the number of records in the second table.

Each of the join types we've examined here serves its own unique purpose. It's also possible to execute an UPDATE statement that uses multiple files; however, this is not accomplished using the JOIN clause. A sub-SELECT must be used to retrieve data from a secondary table or table. There are two distinct scenarios in which you'd use a sub-SELECT: within a criteria expression (WHERE clause) or as part of the value to be updated. In cases where the criteria or a portion of the criteria for records to be updated exists within another table, the solution is to replace the criteria value with an SQL SELECT statement. A good example would be when you want to update a value in an order line detail file based on a value from the order header, as shown in Figure 1.12.

```
UPDATE MYLIB.ORDLINS
     SET ODPURG = 'YES'
     WHERE ODORDR  IN (SELECT OHORDR FROM MYLIB.ORDHEAD
         WHERE OHODAT<20030101)
```

Figure 1.12: This example uses an embedded SQL statement as part of the criteria.

13

In this example, the sub-SELECT will return only records in which the order date from the header is less than 20030101. The WHERE clause from the UPDATE statement will find a match only for those records returned by the sub-SELECT shown. The WHERE clause in the sub-SELECT is able to use values from the file you are updating—in this case, the field ODORDR comes from the file MYLIB.ORDLINS, which is what you're updating. The result is that your update is based on criteria contained in a file other than the file to be updated.

When performing an SQL UPDATE, there are often times when not only a criterion is based on values from another file, but also the value of the field to be updated. A good example would be updating a total quantity on a header record by summarizing the values from the line details. You can do this by using a sub-SELECT in a method similar to that used earlier. Figure 1.13 shows an example of this type of SQL UPDATE.

```
UPDATE MYLIB.ORDHEAD
      SET OHOTOT = (SELECT SUM(ODOQTY) FROM MYLIB.ORDLINS
                     WHERE ODORDR=OHORDR)
      WHERE OHODAT<20030101
```

Figure 1.13: This example uses a sub-SELECT to calculate a field value.

This example uses the sub-SELECT as the target for the SET clause. When the statement is run, the value of the field ODOQTY in the file ORDLINS will be summarized for all records where the value of ODORDR is equal to the field OHORDR from ORDHEAD (the file to be updated). Again, you use a value from the "primary" file, ORDHEAD, within the WHERE clause of the sub-SELECT.

It's important to remember that the sub-SELECT used must return only one value for each record in the file to be updated, meaning that there must be a one-to-one relationship between each record in the file to be updated and the value returned by the sub-SELECT. If not, you'll get an SQL0811 error stating that the result of the SELECT is more than one row. The same would be true when using the sub-SELECT as part of the WHERE clause. This is not a problem in this example because the SUM() function summarizes all records within the ODORDR file that match the criteria.

Both methods can be combined to use the sub-SELECT as part of the SET clause and the WHERE clause. This method can be useful when, for example, you want to recalculate an order total in an order header file by summarizing the line details from the order detail file for customers in a specific region based on a value from a customer master file. Figure 1.14, a modified version of an earlier example, performs this task.

```
UPDATE MYLIB.ORDHEAD
        SET OHOTOT = (SELECT SUM(ODOQTY) FROM MYLIB.ORDLINS
                      WHERE ODORDR=OHORDR)
        WHERE OHCUSN IN(SELECT CMCUSN FROM MYLIB.CUSTMAST
                      WHERE CMREGN='NE' AND CMCUSN=OHCUSN)
```

Figure 1.14: This example uses sub-SELECT for both the criteria and the value.

The WHERE clause used in this SQL statement may be a bit confusing at first. The sub-SELECT statement will return the customer number from the file CUSTMAST only if the value of CMREGN is 'NE'. Placing this sub-SELECT inside of the IN predicate generates a list of values, which are compared to the value of OHCUSN. The sub-SELECT used with the SET clause summarizes the value of the field ODOQTY for all records where the value of the field ODORDR matches the value of OHORDR from ORDHEAD. When this statement is executed, the order total summary will be recalculated for all customers in the region 'NE'. In this example, we are actually using values from two separate tables in addition to the table being updated.

A similar technique can be used with the DELETE statement to remove records from one table based on data in another. In this case, we would be using a sub-SELECT with the WHERE clause to determine which records to delete. The statement in Figure 1.15 illustrates this by using a modified version of an earlier example.

```
DELETE
FROM MYLIB.ORDLINS
        WHERE EXISTS (SELECT OHORDR FROM MYLIB.ORDHEAD
                        WHERE OHORDR=ODORDR AND
                        OHODAT<20030101)
```

Figure 1.15: This example uses sub-SELECT to define the criteria for a DELETE statement.

In this example, we utilized the EXISTS predicate. This function can be used to determine whether any records are returned by a sub-SELECT. If the sub-SELECT returns any rows, the EXISTS predicate will return a value of TRUE; otherwise, a value of FALSE will be returned.

From Language Structure to Functions

In this chapter, we've taken a quick look at the SQL language structure and examined how to perform some specific tasks using SQL. Now that you've reviewed the SQL primer, you're ready to delve into the world of SQL functions.

2

Built-In Functions

As we've already seen, SQL is a powerful tool for manipulating data. Part of what makes the language so powerful is the built-in functions (BIFs). These allow you to perform complex tasks with a single statement within an SQL program. This capability becomes even more powerful when you consider that you can use these functions and procedures within any of the embedded SQL languages or within DB2 Query Manager for creating printed reports.

In this chapter, we'll explore the BIFs included in the DB2 implementation of SQL on the iSeries. Before we begin, however, it's important to understand what the similarities and differences are between a *function* and a *procedure*. These terms are used with SQL in much the same way that they would be used within any other programming language, including ILE RPG. A *function* is a compiled set of statements that performs a required task and returns a value. Functions can be used to perform simple tasks, like calculating or manipulating a value, or more complex tasks, like looking up a value in a database table and returning that value to the caller. A *procedure* is a compiled set of statements that performs a required task but does not return a value. Generally, an SQL *stored procedure* is simply a compiled program that can be called through an SQL call. This gives us the ability to use a compiled program like this from client applications through ADO, ODBC, or JDBC. Let's start by examining the BIFs in DB2 on the iSeries.

Built-In Functions

The SQL BIFs in DB2 can be broken down into two main categories. *Columnar* SQL functions are used to calculate summary-level values. *Scalar* SQL functions are used at a detail level. Since the uses of these two types of functions are distinctly different, we'll examine each group of functions separately.

Columnar Functions

These functions allow you to create total- or subtotal-level summaries. Subtotal-level groupings are defined using the GROUP BY clause. Table 2.1 displays a list of the columnar functions supported in DB2 along with a brief description of their use. This group of functions allows you to summarize data sets.

Table 2.1: DB2 Columnar Functions

Function	Description
AVG	This function returns an average of the field or value on the supplied parameter over the defined data set.
SUM	This function returns the total of the supplied field values within the defined data set.
COUNT	This function determines the number of rows within the defined data set.
COUNT_BIG	This function also returns the number of rows within the defined data set, but it supports more digits than the standard integer value returned by the COUNT function.
MAX	This function returns the maximum value for the field supplied on its parameter within the defined data set.

Table 2.1: DB2 Columnar Functions (continued)

Function	Description
MIN	This function is the opposite of the MAX function. It returns the minimum value within the defined data set.
STDDEV_POP or STDEV	These functions return the standard deviation (or the square root of the variance) of the supplied field value within the defined data set.
VAR_POP or VARIANCE or VAR	These functions return the variance calculated on the supplied field value within the defined data set.

The AVG function calculates the average value of a field within the data set. The following example shows how to use this function to calculate an average item price from an order file.

```
SELECT ITEM, AVG(PRICE)
FROM ORDERDTL
GROUP BY ITEM
```

The GROUP BY clause defines the level at which the values are summarized.

The SUM function performs much as you would assume. It totals the values from the specified field or fields. With many of the columnar functions, it's possible to use multiple fields or values. The example below illustrates this by using the SUM function to calculate the total dollar value of orders from the same order file used in the previous example.

```
SELECT ORDNO, SUM(PRICE * QTY)
FROM ORDERDTL
GROUP BY ORDNO
```

When this example is executed, the value of PRICE * QTY is calculated and then used as our summary field.

The COUNT function can be used to count the number of rows in a group of records within a data set. If we add the COUNT function to the prior example, we can determine the number of order lines that make up each order.

```
SELECT ORDNO, SUM(PRICE * QTY) AS VALUE, COUNT(*) AS LINES
FROM ORDERDTL
GROUP BY ORDNO
HAVING SUM(PRICE * QTY)>0
```

Within this example, you'll notice that we've added the AS modifier to name the field created by each of our functions. You'll also notice that we've added the HAVING clause. It is acceptable to include a columnar function in the HAVING clause of a SELECT statement. In this example, groups will be displayed only if the SUM(PRICE * QTY) is greater than 0.

The COUNT_BIG function works exactly like the COUNT function, but while the COUNT function can only return a value of up to 15 digits, the COUNT_BIG function supports a value of up to 31 digits.

The MIN and MAX functions return the minimum and maximum values for the specified field in a group within a data set. The following example uses these two functions to determine the earliest and latest dates that an item was received.

```
SELECT ITEM, MIN(ORDDATE), MAX(ORDDATE)
FROM RECEIPTS
GROUP BY ITEM
```

While each of these functions is based on the same field, the values returned by the functions can be distinctly different. This statement would return both the earliest and the most recent order date value for each item in the file RECEIPTS.

The functions VAR (or VAR_POP or VARIANCE) and STDDEV (or STDEV_POP) are used for statistical analysis. A variance is calculated by taking the mean of the square root of the difference between the mean value in a series of numbers and each number itself. Figure 2.1 illustrates calculating a variance on the numbers 1, 4, and 13.

$$variance = \frac{(1-6)^2 + (4-6)^2 + (13-6)^2}{3}$$

Figure 2.1: This simple illustration shows the formula to calculate a variance.

In this example, the mean or average value in our series is 6. The difference between the values and 6 is calculated, giving us -5, -2, and 7, respectively. These values are then squared, which results in 25, 4, and 49, respectively. The sum of these values (78) is then divided by the number of values (3), which gives us a variance of 26. The standard deviation is simply the square root of the variance. Using our previous example, we would arrive at a standard deviation of 5.09902. Generally, these two functions are used to give an idea of the range of values that exist within a set of numbers. The different versions of the functions are included for maximum compatibility with other SQL implementations.

As we've seen here, columnar functions give us a way to take volumes of data and summarize them into a form that is more easily analyzed. Next, we'll go through the scalar functions available.

Scalar Functions

Scalar functions allow us to extend existing values within a data set. These functions can be used not only as part of the SELECT list and HAVING clauses, but also as part of file join and WHERE conditions. In addition, they can be used as a part of a GROUP BY or ORDER BY clause. Basically, anywhere that a field name or value can be specified, a scalar function can be used.

DB2 UDB for the iSeries supports more than 150 scalar functions that allow you to control any type of field—from numeric to string to date. Some of these functions will be familiar to you because of their similarity to functions in other common languages. Table 2.2 breaks down these functions into groups based on their use.

Table 2.2: DB2 Scalar Functions

Numeric	String	Date/Time	Logical
ABS	BINARY*	CURDATE	LAND
ACOS	BIT_LENGTH*	CURTIME	LNOT
ANTILOG	CHAR	DATE	LOR
ASIN	CHARACTER_LENGTH	DAY	XOR
ATAN	CHAR_LENGTH	DAYNAME*	
ATANH	CONCAT	DAYOFMONTH	**Other**
ATAN2	DIFFERENCE	DAYOFWEEK	BLOB
BIGINT	DIGITS	DAYOFWEEK_ISO	CLOB
CEILING	GRAPHIC	DAYOFYEAR	COALESCE
COS	INSERT*	DAYS	DATABASE*
COSH	LCASE	EXTRACT*	DATAPARTITIONNAME*
COT	LEFT	HOUR	DATAPARTITIONNUM*
DECIMAL	LENGTH	JULIAN_DAY	DBCLOB
DEGREES	LOCATE	MICROSECOND	DBPARTITIONNAME*
DOUBLE	LOWER	MIDNIGHT_SECONDS	DBPARTITIONNUM*
DOUBLE_PRECISION	LTRIM	MINUTE	DECRYPT_ BINARY*
EXP	OCTET_LENGTH*	MONTH	DECRYPT_ BIT*
FLOAT	POSITION	MONTHNAME*	DECRYPT_CHAR*
FLOOR	POSSTR	NOW	DECRYPT_DB*
INT	REPEAT*	QUARTER	ENCRYPT_RC2*
INTEGER	REPLACE*	SECOND	GETHINT*
LN	RIGHT*	TIME	HASH
LOG10	RTRIM	TIMESTAMP	HASHED_VALUE*

Table 2.2: DB2 Scalar Functions (continued)

Numeric	String	Date/Time	Logical
MOD	SOUNDEX	TIMESTAMP_ISO*	HEX
MULTIPLY_ALT*	SPACE	TIMESTAMPDIFF	IDENTITY_VAL_LOCAL
PI	STRIP	WEEK	IFNULL
POWER	SUBST	WEEK_ISO	MAX
RADIANS	SUBSTRING	YEAR	MIN
RAND	TRANSLATE		NODENAME
REAL	TRIM	**URL**	NULL
REPEAT	UCASE	DLCOMMENT	NULLIF
REPLACE	UPPER	DLLINKTYPE	RRN
ROUND	VARBINARY*	DLURLCOMPLETE	VALUE
SIGN	VARCHAR	DLURLPATH	
SIN	VARGRAPHIC	DLURLPATHONLY	
SINH		DLURLSCHEME	
SMALLINT		DLURLSERVER	
SQRT		DLVALUE	
STRIP			
TAN			
TANH			
TRUNC			
TRUNCATE			
ZONED			

Note: Functions noted by an asterisk (*) indicate new functions added between V5R2 and V5R3.

Let's review the groups of functions one at a time. The first group of functions focuses on numeric operations. You'll probably find that you use these functions more than the other groups.

Numeric Functions

As the grouping suggests, these functions perform operations on numeric fields. The ABS function returns the absolute value of the provided field or value. The following statement is an example of using ABS.

```
SELECT ABS(TRANQT)
       FROM TRANSFILE
```

Assuming the value of the field TRANQT is -25, the value returned would be 25.

The ACOS function converts the supplied value to an arc cosine value. This function performs the opposite operation to the COS function. The value returned is the angle in radians. The following statement shows a sample of the ACOS function.

```
SELECT ACOS(.25)
       FROM MYFILE
```

Using this sample statement, the ACOS function would return 1.318116072.

The COS function returns the cosine value for the provided value. As with the ACOS function, the value returned is an angle in radians. If in the previous example we replaced the ACOS function with the COS function, the value returned would be 0.968912422.

ANTILOG returns the base 10 anti-logarithm value for the provided value. This function performs the opposite operation of the LOG function. When executed, the ANTILOG function will evaluate 10^x where x is the supplied value. The following example calculates the ANTILOG and LOG for the number 3.

```
SELECT ANTILOG(3), LOG(3)
       FROM MYFILE
```

When executed, this function returns 1.0000000000000007E+003 and 4.7712125471966244E-001, respectively. These values converted to decimal would evaluate to 1,000 and .447, respectively.

The ASIN function calculates the arc sine of a given number. This and the SIN function, which calculates the sine of a given number, are opposites to each other. When I refer to two functions as opposites, what I am saying is that the ASIN(SIN(x)) will equal x and the SIN(ASIN(y)) will equal y. The following statement illustrates how these opposite operations work.

```
SELECT DECIMAL(ASIN(.997495),15,5), DECIMAL(SIN(1.5),15,5)
       FROM MYFILE
```

When executed, this statement returns values of 1.5 and .99749, respectively.

Note that we are making use of another function here. The DECIMAL function converts the supplied value to a decimal value. The supplied value can be any numeric format or a character string that evaluates to a number. The second parameter identifies the total length of the returned numeric value. The third parameter defines the precision and the number of decimal places shown. If the second and third optional parameters are omitted, the value returned will have zero decimal places. The example below illustrates using the DECIMAL function to convert a character string representation of a number to a 15-digit numeric field with two decimal places.

```
SELECT DECIMAL('123.159999',15,2)
       FROM MYFILE
```

The value returned by this SELECT statement would be 123.15. You'll notice that the resulting value is not rounded up. Any trailing decimals are simply truncated.

25

A series of functions is available for calculating arc tangent and inverse functions for tangents. The ATAN function calculates the arc tangent of the provided value. Its opposite function, TAN, calculates the tangent for the provided value. The ATANH and TANH functions return the hyperbolic arc tangent and hyperbolic tangent values, respectively. While these functions accept a single parameter between -1 and 1, the ATAN2 function returns the arc tangent based on two provided parameters, which represent x and y coordinates.

```
SELECT DECIMAL(ATAN(.5),15,5), DECIMAL(ATANH(.5),15,5),
       DECIMAL(ATAN2(5,3),15,5)
    FROM MYFILE
```

This example evaluates each of these functions. The values returned would be .46364, .54390, and .54041, respectively. Replacing the first two functions in our example with their opposite functions, the resulting values would be .54630 for the TAN function and .46211 for TANH.

The BIGINT function converts a value to a large integer. This value can be up to 31 numeric positions. The INTEGER and INT functions behave identically (for some functions, multiple versions exist for compatibility purposes). These two functions also convert the supplied value to an integer value, with a length of up to 15 numeric positions. The parameter supplied to the function can be a numeric value that is not an integer or a character value that represents a numeric value. The following sample statement illustrates multiple uses of the BIGINT function.

```
SELECT BIGINT('1250.5575'),BIGINT('1075723489760235'),
       BIGINT(107505230695704321.122585)
    FROM MYFILE
```

When executed, this example will return 1250, 1075723489760235, and 107505230695704321, respectively. Note that our first example illustrates a character representation of a floating point number. The second example shows a character representation of a long integer value, and the third field is a floating point value.

SQL supports two functions for rounding a numeric value to an integer. The CEIL-ING function rounds the supplied value to the next highest integer value. Similarly, the FLOOR function rounds to the first integer value that is less than or equal to the supplied value. The following statement shows a sample of these two functions.

```
SELECT CEILING(25.475), FLOOR(25.575)
       FROM MyFile
```

The first column will return a value of 26, while the second will return 25. These functions allow you to force rounding in one direction or another based on your need.

Many of the geometric functions we've examined return a value that is a representation of an angle in radians. To convert this value to a number of degrees, we can use the DEGREES function. This function accepts a single parameter, which contains the radians value. Below is a sample of using this statement with the COS function.

```
SELECT DECIMAL(DEGREES(COS(.75)),15,5)
       FROM MyFile
```

When this statement is executed, the value returned would be 41.92268 degrees.

The DOUBLE, DOUBLE_PRECISION, and FLOAT functions convert the provided value into a floating point numeric value. The supplied parameter can contain a numeric or character string value. Below is an example of this statement.

```
SELECT DOUBLE(ORDQTY)
       FROM ORDERS
```

Assuming that the field of ORDQTY contained a value of 65.490, the value returned by any of these three functions would be $6.5489999999999995E+001$.

The EXP function raises the natural logarithm "e" (approximately 2.71828182846) to the power specified on the supplied parameter. The statement below illustrates the use of this function.

```
SELECT EXP(ORDQTY)
       FROM ORDERS
```

If the value of the field ORDQTY was 6, the value returned by this function would be 403.428793492735110.

The LN function is the opposite function to the EXP function; it returns the natural logarithm for the supplied value. The example below illustrates the use of this function.

```
SELECT LN(403.428793492735110)
       FROM MYFILE
```

When executed, this statement returns a value of 6.

Similarly the LOG10 function returns the common logarithm (base 10) of the supplied value. The example below returns a value of 3.

```
SELECT LOG10(1000)
       FROM MYFILE
```

The MOD function calculates a remainder when the first parameter is divided by the second. The sample statement below illustrates how this function is used.

```
SELECT MOD(20,3)
       FROM MYFILE
```

In this example, 20 divided by 3 evaluates to 6 with a remainder of 2. As a result, 2 is the value returned by the function.

The MULTIPLY_ALT function is used as an alternative to performing multiplication operations using the asterisk (*) operator. The two values provided are multiplied by one another.

```
SELECT MULTIPLY_ALT(12,5)
       FROM MYFILE
```

As one might expect, this example returns a value of 60.

The PI function evaluates the value of pi (3.141592653589793). The example below calculates the circumference of a circle whose diameter is 5.

```
SELECT PI()*5
        FROM MYFILE
```

The result returned when this statement is executed is 15.7.

String Functions

Character strings and values can be manipulated using the string functions supported in SQL.

The CHAR function allows us to convert other field types to a character string value. When using this function, the first parameter defines the value to be converted. The second parameter is defined differently, depending on what type of value is identified by the first parameter. When a DATE or TIME field is being converted, the second parameter identifies the format for the converted date. Table 2.3 contains a list of the possible values.

Table 2.3: The CHAR Function Date Formats

Date Type	String Functions	Format
ISO	Industry Standards Organization format	(yyyy-mm-dd)
USA	USA date format	(mm/dd/yyyy)
EUR	European standard format	(dd.mm.yyyy)
JIS	Japanese Industrial Standard	(yyyy-mm-dd)
LOCAL	Based on the time/date format defined on the server	

When the CHAR function is used on a character or graphic field, the second parameter identifies the length of the resulting string from 1 to 32766. When the

CHAR function is used on an integer field, the second parameter is not used. When it's used on other numeric fields, the value should be specified as a field containing the single character to be used in place of the decimal point when the field is converted. The following statement shows samples of each of these conversions.

```
SELECT CHAR(DATE('12/12/2004'),ISO), CHAR('ABCDEFGHIJK',6),
    CHAR(123.45, ',')
        FROM SYSIBM.SYSDUMMY1
```

This statement uses the DATE function, which we'll examine later, to arrive at a date value. When executed, the statement will return values of 2004-12-12, ABCDEF, and 123,45. The date value is converted from USA format to ISO format. The character string is truncated to 6 characters based on the second parameter. With our third column, the decimal point is replaced by a comma.

The CHAR_LENGTH, CHARACTER_LENGTH, and LENGTH functions determine the length of a character string. When the parameter specified is a field name, the length of the field itself is returned. If a string literal is specified, the full length of that string, including trailing blanks, is returned. Following is a sample of using this function.

```
SELECT CHAR_LENGTH('123456      '), CHAR_LENGTH('123456')
        FROM SYSIBM.SYSDUMMY1
```

When this statement is executed, the first column returns a value of 12, while the second column returns a value of 6. The VARCHAR function is used in the same way that CHAR is used except that the value returned is a VARCHAR field.

To join two string expressions into one, we use the CONCAT function. The first parameter specified is joined with the second parameter specified in the same way that two strings can be joined, using the double bar (||) concatenation operator. Below is a sample of using this function.

```
SELECT CONCAT('ABC','123'), 'ABC' || '123'
        FROM SYSIBM.SYSDUMMY1
```

When this statement is executed, both columns return a value of ABC123.

The DIFFERENCE function determines how similar two string values are, based on the SOUNDEX function. To examine the DIFFERENCE function, we should first examine the SOUNDEX function itself. This function returns a four-character value, which is used to analyze the sound of a word. The example below returns the SOUNDEX values for two similar words.

```
SELECT SOUNDEX('TREE'), SOUNDEX('TRACE')
       FROM SYSIBM.SYSDUMMY1
```

Upon execution of this statement, the first column returns a value of T600, and the second returns a value of T620. If we change the string supplied to the first SOUNDEX function to 'TREES', the two values match. The DIFFERENCE function uses this logic to compare the two strings provided to the function. The value returned is a numeric value from 0 to 4, where 4 is the closest to a match and 0 is the furthest from a match. The statement below shows examples of each of the values.

```
SELECT DIFFERENCE('TREES','TRACE'),
       DIFFERENCE('TREE','TRACE'),
       DIFFERENCE('TIES','TRACE'),
       DIFFERENCE('APPLE','TRACE')
       FROM SYSIBM.SYSDUMMY1
```

When this statement is executed, the values 4, 3, 2, and 1 will be returned. These two functions can be very useful, for example, when searching for a customer name where you are unsure of the spelling. The statement below gives an example of this.

```
SELECT CUSLNM, CUSFNM, CUSADD, CUSCTY, CUSSTE, CUSPHN
       FROM CUSNAMES
       WHERE DIFFERENCE(CUSLNM, 'JONSON')=4
```

Using this example, records will be returned for the names JOHNSON, JOHNSEN, and JENSEN, but not for JONES. You can use a lower numeric value to make the search less sensitive.

The DIGITS function is similar to the CHAR function. This function converts a numeric value to a character string value. The value returned to the string is unsigned, meaning that it is based on the absolute value of the numeric value supplied. The decimal point is also excluded from the string value. The statement below illustrates the use of this function.

```
SELECT DIGITS(-10123.858)
       FROM SYSIBM.SYSDUMMY1
```

When executed, this statement returns a value of 10123858. This function can be useful when you need to substring portions of a numeric field. For example, the following statement will take a date stored in an 8-digit numeric field as 20041231 and convert it to a displayable string representation of the date in mm/dd/yyyy format.

```
SELECT SUBSTR(DIGITS(DTEFLD),5,2) || '/' ||
       SUBSTR(DIGITS(DTEFLD),7,2) || '/' ||
       SUBSTR(DIGITS(DTEFLD),1,4)
       FROM MYFILE
```

Assuming that the value of DTEFLD is 20041231, when this statement is executed, a value of '12/31/2004' is returned.

The INSERT function inserts a specified string into a source string, starting at a specified position, while deleting the number of characters specified as length. The first parameter used on this function defines the source string. The second parameter defines the starting position at which the insertion is to occur within that source string. The third parameter defines the number of characters from the start position to delete from the source string prior to insertion. The final parameter identifies the string to be inserted. Below is an example of the syntax for this function.

```
SELECT INSERT('ABCDEF' ,3, 4, 'OUT')
       SYSIBM.SYSDUMMY1
```

When this statement is executed, the value 'ABOUT' is returned. If the string to be inserted is defined as null, the characters defined by the start position and length will be removed from the string altogether.

The GRAPHIC and VARGRAPHIC functions convert from character or numeric data to a value compatible with double-byte character data as is used for the Chinese or Japanese language. The result of either of these functions will be a field that is either a GRAPHIC or VARGRAPHIC data type, respectively. The statement below illustrates the use of both of these functions.

```
SELECT GRAPHIC('HELLO'), VARGRAPHIC('HELLO')
       FROM SYSIBM.SYSDUMMY1
```

When this statement is executed, both columns return the value 'âHâEâLâLâO'.

The LCASE and LOWER functions convert the provided string to a lowercase representation of the same string. Below is an example of this function.

```
SELECT LCASE('ABC123')
       FROM SYSIBM.SYSDUMMY1
```

When executed, this statement returns a value of 'abc123'.

Similarly, the functions UCASE and UPPER convert a string to uppercase. Below is a sample of the UPPER function.

```
SELECT UPPER('Mike Faust')
       FROM SYSIBM.SYSDUMMY1
```

When this statement is executed, the value 'MIKE FAUST' is returned.

The LEFT function extracts a specified number of characters from the left side of the provided string value. The first parameter identifies the source string, while the second defines the number of characters to be extracted. Below is a sample statement using this function.

```
SELECT LEFT('ABC123', 3)
       FROM SYSIBM.SYSDUMMY1
```

This statement will return the value 'ABC' when executed.

The RIGHT function is similar to this function with the exception that it extracts from the right side of the defined string. Below is a modified version of the previous statement using RIGHT.

```
SELECT RIGHT('ABC123', 3)
       FROM SYSIBM.SYSDUMMY1
```

When this statement is executed, the value '123' is returned.

The SUBSTR (or SUBSTRING) function is also used to extract characters from a source string. This function, however, accepts three parameters: The first is the source string, the second defines the starting position for the characters to be extracted, and the third defines the number of characters to be extracted. The statement below shows an example of this function.

```
SELECT SUBSTR('ABC123', 3, 2)
       FROM SYSIBM.SYSDUMMY1
```

When executed, this statement returns a value of 'C1'.

The LOCATE function searches for the string defined on its first parameter within the source string defined on its second. An optional third parameter can be specified to identify the start point within the source string to search. Below is an example of this function's use.

```
SELECT LOCATE('AB', 'ABCABDABE'), LOCATE('AB', 'ABCABDABE', 3)
       FROM SYSIBM.SYSDUMMY1
```

When this statement is executed, the first column returns a value of 1. The second column returns a value of 2, which is the location where the string is found, taking the start position into consideration. To determine the actual start position in this case, we need to take the start position value (3), add the value returned (2), and subtract 1, giving us a value of 4.

The POSSTR and POSITION functions perform a similar function to LOCATE. However, these functions accept only the search string and source string values. A start position cannot be specified with these functions. Below is an example.

```
SELECT POSITION('AB' IN 'BCABDABE'), POSSTR('BCABDABE', 'AB')
       FROM SYSIBM.SYSDUMMY1
```

When this statement is executed, both of these functions return a value of 3.

We can remove any leading blanks from a string value using the LTRIM function. This function removes all blank spaces from the left side of the supplied string value, effectively left-adjusting that string. Below is a sample of this function.

```
SELECT LENGTH(LTRIM('   ABC'))
       FROM SYSIBM.SYSDUMMY1
```

To illustrate that the resulting string has been changed, I've combined the LENGTH function with the LTRIM function. When executed, this statement returns a value of 3.

Similarly, the RTRIM function removes all trailing blanks from the specified string. The example below illustrates this function's use.

```
SELECT LENGTH(RTRIM('ABC 123      '))
       FROM SYSIBM.SYSDUMMY1
```

When this statement is executed, the trailing blanks will be removed, and a value of 7 is returned. Note that the embedded blank character is not affected.

The TRIM and STRIP functions also remove characters from a specified string, but both have more functionality than the other two functions. When these functions are used with a source string only, the value returned is stripped of both leading and trailing blanks. An example of this is shown below.

```
SELECT LENGTH(TRIM('   1234   '))
       FROM SYSIBM.SYSDUMMY1
```

When this statement is executed, the value 4 is returned. Optional modifiers allow us to use the TRIM function to remove leading and/or trailing blanks or other characters from the supplied string. The example below can be used to remove leading zeros from the defined string.

```
SELECT TRIM(LEADING '0' FROM '000123400'),
       TRIM(TRAILING '0' FROM '000123400'),
       TRIM(BOTH '0' FROM '000123400')
FROM SYSIBM.SYSDUMMY1
```

When this statement is executed, values returned are '123400', '0001234', and '1234', respectively.

The REPEAT function creates a string containing the expression supplied on the first parameter repeated the number of times defined on the second. The statement below illustrates this statement's use.

```
SELECT REPEAT('A1B2C3', 3)
       FROM SYSIBM.SYSDUMMY1
```

When executed, this statement returns a value of 'A1B2C3A1B2C3A1B2C3'.

Similarly, the SPACE function returns a number of blank spaces as specified on the required parameter. The statement below illustrates the use of this function.

```
SELECT SPACE(32)
       FROM SYSIBM.SYSDUMMY1
```

This statement returns a string value containing 32 blank spaces.

The REPLACE function allows us to replace a search string specified on the first parameter within a source string specified on the second parameter with the replacement string specified on the third. The statement below shows four examples of different uses for this statement.

```
SELECT REPLACE('XY', 'XYZ', 'BI'), REPLACE('XY', 'XYZ', ''),
       REPLACE('XY', 'XYZ', 'JAZ'), REPLACE('XY', 'ABC', 'DE'),
       FROM SYSIBM.SYSDUMMY1
```

When this statement is executed, the first column will replace 'XY' in 'XYZ' with 'BI', resulting in 'BIZ'. The second column will replace 'XY' in 'XYZ' with a zero length string, resulting in 'Z'. The third column replaces 'XY' in 'XYZ' with 'JAZ', resulting in 'JAZZ'. Finally, the fourth column doesn't locate 'XY' in 'ABC' and as a result returns the original value of 'ABC'.

Date/Time Functions

SQL contains a set of built-in functions that allow us to manipulate fields containing date and/or time values.

The functions CURDATE and CURTIME allow us to retrieve the current date and current time, respectively. Both functions have no parameters. The statement below shows a sample of using these functions within an INSERT statement.

```
INSERT INTO TRANS(ITEM, QTY, TRNDTE, TRNTIM)
        VALUES('ABC123', 5000, CURDATE(), CURTIME())
```

This statement adds a record to the table named TRANS, which contains four fields. The last two fields represent the date and time of the transaction being added. The DATE function converts a string representation of a date to a date value. We used this function earlier when examining the CHAR function. The date supplied to the DATE function must be a value date in the format as defined for the job. If the job date format is ISO, then a date in the format yyyy-mm-dd must be supplied. The statement below uses this function combined with the CURDATE function.

```
SELECT *
        FROM MYFILE
        WHERE CURDATE>DATE(STRDTE)
```

Assuming that the field MYFILE has a field called STRDTE stored in the date format defined for the current job, this statement will select all records for dates earlier than the current date.

Similarly, the TIME function converts a time stored in a string to a time value. The statement below illustrates the use of this function.

```
SELECT TIME('12.00.00') AS Noon
       FROM SYSIBM.SYSDUMMY1
```

When this statement is executed, the value returned is '12:00:00'. Note that the time separator has been changed from the decimal point to the colon character. This is based on the value defined for the time separator on the job.

A group of functions allows us to extract a given part of a date or time value. The DAY, WEEK, MONTH, QUARTER, and YEAR functions extract the portion of a date field suggested by their name. The example below illustrates this by selecting each component of the CURDATE value.

```
SELECT DAY(CURDATE()), WEEK(CURDATE()), MONTH(CURDATE()),
       QUARTER(CURDATE()), YEAR(CURDATE())
       FROM SYSIBM.SYSDUMMY1
```

When executed, this statement returns columns containing the current date (1 thru 31), week number (1 thru 54), month number (1 thru 12), quarter number (1 thru 4), and year number ().

Similarly, a set of time functions allows us to extract pieces of a time value. WEEK defines the week as starting on Sunday. January 1 always falls in week 1. As an alternative to WEEK, SQL also supports a WEEK_ISO function. This function returns a value from 1 to 53. For WEEK_ISO, the week begins on Monday and is defined as the first week containing a Thursday. This means that if January 1 falls on a Friday, Saturday, or Sunday, then week 1 will be the following week.

The DAYOFWEEK and DAYOFWEEK_ISO functions return the day of the week from 1 to 7. The difference between these two functions is that the DAY-OFWEEK value of 1 indicates Sunday, and the DAYOFWEEK_ISO value of 1 indicates Monday.

Similarly, the DAYOFMONTH function returns the day within the month (1 to 31) for the supplied date value. This function is similar to the DAY function.

38

The DAYOFYEAR function returns a value from 1 to 366 that identifies the day of the year for the supplied date.

The DAYNAME function returns a string containing the name of the day of the week for the supplied date value. The example below illustrates these functions.

```
SELECT DAYOFMONTH(CURDATE()), DAYOFYEAR(CURDATE()), DAYNAME
    (CURDATE()),
        FROM SYSIBM.SYSDUMMY1
```

If this statement is executed on April 15, 2005, the values returned will be '15', '105', and 'Friday'.

SQL also supports functions to allow us to extract pieces of a time field. The functions HOUR, MINUTE, SECOND, and MICROSECOND each extract the portion of the specified time value indicated by their names. Assuming that the value provided to the HOUR function is a time or timestamp or a character representation of a time, the value returned will be between 0 and 24. Each of these functions accepts a time value, a timestamp value, or a string representation of a time. The statement below extracts the hour, minute, and second of the time 12:15:45.

```
SELECT HOUR('12:15:45'), MINUTE('12:15:45'), SECOND('12:15:45')
        FROM SYSIBM.SYSDUMMY1
```

When executed, this statement returns values of '12', '15', and '45', respectively.

The EXTRACT function performs a similar function to each of the individual time and date extraction functions. The first parameter specifies the portion of the date/time value to be extracted. Values of YEAR, MONTH, DAY, HOUR, MINUTE, and SECOND are valid for this parameter. The second parameter supplies the date, time, or timestamp value from which the data is to be extracted. The sample statement below extracts the hour from the current time.

```
SELECT EXTRACT(HOUR, '12:15:45')
       FROM SYSIBM.SYSDUMMY1
```

When this statement is executed, a value of 12 is returned.

The JULIAN_DAY function returns a value representing the number of days since the start of the Julian calendar (1/1/4713 B.C.). The statement below illustrates the use of this function.

```
SELECT JULIAN_DAY('12/31/2005')
       FROM SYSIBM.SYSDUMMY1
```

When executed, this statement returns the value 2453736.

The MIDNIGHT_SECONDS function is similar to JULIAN_DAY. This function returns the number of seconds between midnight and the time provided to the function's parameter. The statement below illustrates the use of this function.

```
SELECT MIDNIGHT_SECONDS('12:30:00')
       FROM SYSIBM.SYSDUMMY1
```

When this statement is executed, a value of 45000 seconds is returned.

The TIMESTAMP function converts string representations of a timestamp or date and time values to a timestamp value. The statement below illustrates two different uses of this statement.

```
SELECT TIMESTAMP(DATE('12/31/2005'),TIME('12:15:00')),
       TIMESTAMP('2005-12-31-12.15.00.000000')
       FROM SYSIBM.SYSDUMMY1
```

When executed, this statement returns timestamp values of 2005-12-31-12.15.00.000000 for both columns. Note that the string representation of the timestamp is specified in the format yyyy-mm-dd-hh.mn.ss.milsec.

The TIMESTAMPDIFF function allows us to express the difference between two timestamps. The first parameter is an integer value used to identify the interval in which the difference between the timestamps should be given. Table 2.4 gives a list of the possible values for this parameter.

Table 2.4: TIMESTAMPDIFF Values

Value	Time Interval	Value	Time Interval
1	Microseconds	32	Weeks
2	Seconds	64	Months
4	Minutes	128	Quarters
8	Hours	256	Years
16	Days		

The second parameter is a 22-character string containing the result of a subtraction operation performed on two timestamp values. The SQL statement below shows how this is accomplished.

```
SELECT TIMESTAMPDIFF(8, CAST(NOW() - TIMESTAMP(
       '2005-01-01-00.00.00.000000') AS CHAR(22)))
       FROM SYSIBM.SYSDUMMY1
```

When this statement is executed, it returns the number of hours between 1/1/2005 at midnight and the current time.

Similarly, the DAYS function converts a given date or timestamp value or a string representation of either of those into a number of days. Generally, this function is used to determine duration in days. The example below illustrates using this function to perform duration-based calculations.

```
SELECT DAYS(ENDATE)-DAYS(STDATE), DATE(DAYS(NOW()) + 5)
       FROM SYSIBM.SYSDUMMY1
```

Assuming that the field ENDATE is 12/31/2005 and STDATE is 6/15/2005, the value returned for this column will be 199. The second example uses the DATE function to convert the DAYS value (plus our increment of 5 additional days) back to a date format. When the statement is executed, this column will result in the current date plus five days.

Datalink Functions

Datalink fields and values allow us to define links from within our database to files outside of our database. These links are defined using URL addressing. They can be files stored on an FTP server (http://ftp.ibm.com/anyfile.txt), on a Web server (http://www.geocities.com/mikeffaust/index.html), or in a local or network share accessible file (file://c:\myfile.txt). The datalink field contains the datalink value itself in addition to an optional comment.

The DLVALUE function creates a datalink value from the string defined on the function's first parameter. The optional second parameter defines the type of link being created. Currently, the only value supported is the value 'URL'. The optional third parameter defines the comment associated with the datalink. The statement below is a sample of using the DLVALUE function.

```
INSERT INTO MYLIB.WEBPAGES(WEBSTE)
   VALUES(DLVALUE('http://www.geocities.com/mikeffaust/ index.html',
   'URL', 'Mike Faust's Tips Website'))
```

When this statement is executed, a datalink value is created for the Web page shown. The datalink comment is set to "Mike Faust's Tips Website."

In addition to the DLVALUE function, several other functions can be used to read information about a given datalink value. The DLCOMMENT function reads the comment from an associated datalink value. This function's only parameter is the name of the datalink field or a datalink value. The statement below shows an example of using this function in a SELECT statement.

```
SELECT DLCOMMENT(WEBSTE)
   FROM MYLIB.WEBPAGES
```

When executed, this statement returns a list containing the comment data for the datalink field WEBSTE in each record of our table. Using our earlier example, this statement would return "Mike Faust's Tips Website."

The DLLINKTYPE function returns the link type for the datalink value provided on the function's first parameter. The example below illustrates how this function is used.

```
SELECT DLLINKTYPE(WEBSTE)
       FROM MYLIB.WEBPAGES
```

Since 'URL' is the only value link type currently supported on DB2, this function should always return the value 'URL'.

The DLURLCOMPLETE function returns the full URL from the supplied datalink value. The statement below illustrates the use of this function.

```
SELECT DLURLCOMPLETE(WEBSTE)
       FROM MYLIB.WEBPAGES
```

Using the data from our previous example, when this statement is executed, the URL 'HTTP://WWW.GEOCITIES.COM/DEFAULT/MIKEFFAUST/INDEX.HTML' is returned. The datalink value is always returned as an uppercase representation of the value supplied.

The DLURLPATH function returns the path and file portion of a datalink value, meaning that it strips out the server name portion of the URL. The sample statement below illustrates the use of this function.

```
SELECT DLURLPATH(WEBSTE)
       FROM MYLIB.WEBPAGES
```

Again using our earlier sample data, when this statement is run, the value returned will be '/DEFAULT/MIKEFFAUST/INDEX.HTML'. The result of this function can include a file access token as a series of asterisks where appropriate.

The DLURLPATHONLY function also returns the path and file portion of a datalink URL but does not include file access tokens.

The DLURLSCHEME function returns the scheme for the datalink provided. This value identifies the type of URL being provided. The sample statement below illustrates the use of this function.

```
SELECT DLURLSCHEME(DLVALUE('https://192.168.50.11/myfile.txt'))
       FROM SYSIBM.SYSDUMMY1
```

When this statement is executed, the value 'HTTPS' is returned.

The DLURLSERVER function returns the portion of the URL associated with the datalink value provided that identifies the server containing the linked document. The sample below shows how this function is used.

```
SELECT
DLURLSERVER(DLVALUE('http://www.geocities.com/mikeffaust/index.html'))
       FROM SYSIBM.SYSDUMMY1
```

When executed, this statement returns the value 'WWW.GEOCITIES.COM'.

Combined, these functions give you full control of a datalink field.

Logic Functions

The logical functions in DB2 SQL allow us to perform AND and OR operations on supplied values. The LAND function accepts two or more string values and performs a logical AND on those two strings. Below is a sample of this statement's use.

```
SELECT HEX('HELLO!'), HEX('FELLOW'), HEX(LAND('HELLO!', 'FELLOW'))
       FROM SYSIBM.SYSDUMMY1
```

This statement takes the string HELLO! and does a logical AND with FELLOW. To get a better idea of the actual function being performed, I've shown each of the values in hex before the AND, while also converting the result of the AND function to hex. The result returned for the three columns is x'C8C5D3D3D65A', x'C6C5D3D3D6E6', and x'C0C5D3D3D642', respectively.

The LNOT function returns the logical NOT value for the provided string expression. The statement below uses this statement to evaluate the logical NOT for the hex value 'FF'.

```
SELECT HEX(LNOT(x'FF'))
       FROM SYSIBM.SYSDUMMY1
```

Note that again I use the HEX function to convert the value returned to hex for viewing. When executed, this statement returns the value '00'.

The LOR function returns the logical OR value for the supplied string expressions. The sample below calculates the logical OR for hex values '3C' and 'C3'.

```
SELECT HEX(LOR(x'3C', x'C3'))
       FROM SYSIBM.SYSDUMMY1
```

Once again, I convert the resulting value to a hex value for easy viewing. When this statement is executed, the result returned will be the hex value 'FF'.

The XOR function returns the logical XOR value for the provided string values. The example below illustrates this function's use.

```
SELECT HEX(XOR(x'FC', x'3F'))
       FROM SYSIBM.SYSDUMMY1
```

As you can see, we are again using hex values in this example, this time calculating the XOR value for hex 'FC' and hex '3F'. The resulting value returned is the hex value 'C3'.

Miscellaneous Functions

The remaining functions fall into what I'll call "other" functions. The BLOB, CLOB, and DBCLOB functions are used to store large object (LOB) data types, such as image files, sound files, videos, or other documents, each of which can have up to 2 gigabytes of data. The BLOB function is used to access a binary LOB. CLOB is used with single-byte character LOBs, and DBCLOB is used with LOBs stored as double-byte character. Each of these functions converts a character string into a LOB.

The first parameter on the function contains the string data. The second parameter, which is optional, provides the length of the LOB to be created.

These functions are usually used to append data to an existing LOB value. The following sample statement illustrates this using the BLOB function.

```
SELECT BLOB('This is LOB Data' CONCAT MYBLOB)
       FROM MYFILE
```

When this statement is executed, the column defined using our function will contain the text shown in addition to the object stored in the field MYBLOB. The value returned by this function will show '*POINTER', indicating that the value is a pointer to the location of the object itself. The same syntax is true for the CLOB and DBCLOB functions.

The COALESCE and IFNULL functions return the first non-null value in the list of supplied parameters. The example below illustrates the use of this function to return a zero value if the value of the field COSTAM is null.

```
SELECT IFNULL(COSTFILE.COSTAM,0) AS COST
       FROM MYFILE LEFT JOIN COSTFILE ON MYFILE.ITEM =
       COSTFILE.ITEM
```

Note that in this example I am using a left join expression to indicate that all records from the file on the left side of the join should be included and any matching records from the table on the right side of the expression should be included. This means that we can have records where no record is returned for the table COSTFILE. In that situation, the value of the field COSTFILE.COSTAM will be null. This function prevents the statement from returning a null value for this column.

The NULLIF function performs the opposite function to IFNULL. NULLIF returns a null value if the two values provided on the function's parameters are equal. The statement below makes use of this function.

```
SELECT NULLIF(COST1,0)
       FROM MYTABLE
```

When this example is executed, the function will return null for any case where COST1 is 0; otherwise, the function will return the value of COST1.

The VALUE function returns the first value in the list of values supplied that does not evaluate to NULL. Ultimately, this is similar to IFNULL with additional functionality. The statement below illustrates this function's use.

```
SELECT VALUE(PRICEFILE.PRICE, COSTFILE.COSTAM, 0) AS DOLLARS
       FROM MYFILE LEFT JOIN COSTFILE ON MYFILE.ITEM =
   COSTFILE.ITEM LEFT JOIN PRICEFILE ON MYFILE.ITEM =
   PRICEFILE.ITEM
```

When this statement is executed, the first non-null value is returned. If either of the tables COSTFILE or PRICEFILE does not contain a matching item record, the value of their fields will evaluate to null. If both fields evaluate to null, a value of 0 is returned.

The DATABASE function returns the name of the current SQL database. This value will generally be the system name of your iSeries or i5. This function has no parameters. The statement below illustrates its use.

```
SELECT DATABASE()
       FROM SYSIBM.SYSDUMMY1
```

When this statement is executed, a value representing the name of the current database is returned.

The DATAPARTITIONNAME function returns the data partition name for each row returned by a statement. Partitioning allows us to store data in multiple members yet treat those members as a single table from within SQL. The

DATAPARTITIONNAME value returned is the name of the partition or member containing the current row of data. Similarly, the DATAPARTITIONNUM function determines the partition number containing the current row. The statement below returns the partition name and number for each row in the table supplied on the first parameter.

```
SELECT DATAPARTITIONNAME(S1), DATAPARTITIONNUM(S1)
       FROM SYSIBM.SYSDUMMY1 S1
```

While the DBPARTITIONNAME and DBPARTITIONNUM functions look similar to the two I've just explained, they are not the same functions. These two functions give the partition names related to data spread across multiple systems. The DBPARTITIONNAME function returns the relational database name containing the current row, and the NODENAME function performs the exact same task. The DBPARTITIONNUM function returns the database partition number for the current row. If the table defined on the function's parameter is not a distributed table, the function returns a value of 0. The following statement illustrates the use of these two functions.

```
SELECT DBPARTITIONNAME(S1), DBPARTITIONNUM(S1)
       FROM SYSIBM.SYSDUMMY1 S1
```

DB2 SQL supports a set of functions for encrypting and decrypting data. The ENCRYPT_RC2 function uses the RC2 encryption algorithm to encrypt the data supplied on its first parameter. This function supports two additional parameters that define a password, which is required to decrypt the data, and a hint value to assist in retrieving a lost password. A password can also be specified using the SET ENCRYPTION PASSWORD statement. The following statement is an example of using the ENCRYPT_RC2 function to insert encrypted account number values into a table.

```
INSERT INTO ACCOUNTS(ACCTNM)
       VALUES(ENCRYPT_RC2('123456789', 'EAGLE', 'TALON')
```

When executed, this statement will insert a row containing the encrypted value 123456789 with a password of EAGLE and a hint value of TALON. To decrypt a value encrypted in this method, we can choose from the following functions.

1. DECRYPT_BIT decrypts bit data.

2. DECRYPT_BINARY decrypts binary data.

3. DECRYPT_CHAR decrypts single-byte character data.

4. DECRYPT_DB decrypts double-byte character data.

The first parameter for each of these functions represents the field containing the encrypted data. The second parameter contains the encryption password or the special value DEFAULT, which identifies that the password defined using SET ENCRYPTION PASSWORD statement should be used. The optional third parameter can be used with single- and double-byte character fields to define the code page. The statement below illustrates using the DECRYPT_CHAR function to decrypt the value inserted in the previous example.

```
SELECT DECRYPT_CHAR(ACCTNM, 'EAGLE')
       FROM ACCOUNTS
```

When this statement is executed, the value '123456789' is returned.

The GETHINT function retrieves the hint text for the provided encryption field. The statement below illustrates using this function with the sample data we created earlier.

```
SELECT GETHINT(ACCTNM)
       FROM ACCOUNTS
```

When executed, this statement returns the value 'TALON'.

The HASH function returns a value indicating the partition number containing the values specified. The value returned is an integer between 0 and 1023. Below is a sample of this statement.

```
SELECT HASH(IBMREQD)
       FROM SYSIBM.SYSDUMMY1
```

Similarly, the HASHED_VALUE function returns the partition number. However, this function returns the value based on the current row in the table specified on the function's only parameter. Again, the value returned is an integer number between 0 and 1023. Below is a sample of this statement. Note the S1 identifier after the table name, which is used as an alias for this table in the HASH function.

```
SELECT HASH(S1)
      FROM SYSIBM.SYSDUMMY1 S1
```

We used the HEX function in earlier examples. This function returns a hexadecimal representation of a string value. The statement below illustrates using this function to convert three different values to hex.

```
SELECT HEX(12), HEX('HELLO'), HEX(DATE('12/15/2005'))
      FROM SYSIBM.SYSDUMMY1
```

This example converts a numeric value, a string value, and a date value to hexadecimal. When executed, this statement returns x'0000000C', x'C8C5D3D3D6', and x'002570D8', respectively, for the columns above.

The function IDENTITY_VAL_LOCAL determines the most recent value of an identity column. The statement below assumes that the table MYTABLE contains an identity column defined using the modifiers "INTEGER GENERATED ALWAYS AS IDENTITY" when creating the column on the CREATE TABLE statement.

```
SELECT IDENTITY_VAL_LOCAL()
      FROM MYTABLE
```

Assuming that the last record added to MYTABLE had an identity column value of 15, this function would return 15.

The RRN function is somewhat similar to the IDENTITY_VAL_LOCAL function. It returns the relative record number for the current record in the table defined on the function's single parameter. The example below illustrates the use of the RRN function.

```
SELECT RRN(S1)
        FROM SYSIBM.SYSDUMMY1 S1
```

When executed on the sample table SYSIBM.SYSDUMMY1, this function returns a single record showing a value of 1. If this statement is executed on a larger table, a value is returned for each record in the table.

The MAX and MIN scalar functions perform similar tasks to their columnar cousins. These two functions return the highest value in the list of values and/or fields provided on the function's parameters. The statement below illustrates the use of both functions.

```
SELECT MIN(COST1, COST2, COST3), MAX(COST1, COST2, COST3)
        FROM MYTABLE
```

When this statement is executed, the first column will return a value representing the lowest of the fields COST1, COST2, and COST3. The second will return the greatest of the fields COST1, COST2, and COST3.

Functions vs. Procedures

Now that you have a good understanding of built-in functions and what they can do, it's time to move on to chapter 3 to learn more about stored procedures.

Creating Custom Stored Procedures

Structured Query Language (SQL) is often thought of as a "query tool." The key word in the name, however, is "language." And like other programming languages, SQL can be used to create complex applications. In this chapter, we'll look at using SQL to create our own stored procedures as well as external stored procedures using other languages, which will allow you to execute any program on the iSeries from within SQL.

Create Procedure

The essential element of the SQL stored procedure language is the CREATE PROCEDURE statement. This statement is used to identify the type of procedure we're creating. The basic form for this statement is shown below.

```
CREATE PROCEDURE proc-name (parm list) LANGUAGE language-identifier
option-list
```

This form is common between external stored procedures—that is, procedures created in another programming language—and SQL stored procedures. External stored procedures utilize the EXTERNAL NAME option to define the name of the external program to be used with this procedure. In both external and SQL stored procedures, the LANGUAGE identifier defines the language used for the stored procedure. These are the possible values for this parameter:

- C
- C++
- COBOL
- COBOLLE
- FORTRAN
- JAVA
- PLI
- REXX
- RPG
- RPGLE
- SQL

When we create an SQL stored procedure, the SQL code that makes up the procedure is defined along with the CREATE PROCEDURE statement itself. When identifying parameters for use with our procedure, each parameter is defined using one of the modifiers IN, OUT, or INOUT, followed by the parameter name and the data type associated with the parameter. IN identifies an input parameter, while OUT identifies a parameter sent back to the calling application. INOUT identifies a parameter that is used for both input and output. The code segment below illustrates parameter definition.

```
CREATE PROCEDURE MYPROC (IN InputParm DEC(15,0), OUT OutputParm
CHAR(50));
```

This code segment defines a single input parameter as a decimal field with a length of 15 characters and 0 decimal places along with a single output parameter as a 50-character string field.

The PARAMETER STYLE option, which is exclusive to external stored procedures, identifies the method used to pass parameters to the procedure. PARAMETER STYLE SQL passes some additional parameters to the procedure to be called. In addition to the parameters defined on the CREATE PROCEDURE statement, this style passes a number of indicator fields equal to the number of procedure parameters. SQL STYLE also passes the SQLSTATE value in a five-character string field. It passes an input parameter with a type of VARCHAR and a length of 517 characters, too. This parameter contains the fully qualified procedure name (including the library). The next parameter, which is also an input VARCHAR field, has a length of 128. The final parameter passed is an output VARCHAR parameter that is 70 characters in length.

PARAMETER STYLE DB2SQL includes all of the parameters of PARAMETER STYLE SQL as well as an optional parameter that may contain the DBINFO data structure.

PARAMETER STYLE DB2GENERAL is used with an external function written in Java. The parameters are passed in a manner compatible with Java applications. Similarly, PARAMETER STYLE JAVA can also be specified for use with Java procedures. These parameter styles are not valid for use with external procedures that are not Java applications.

PARAMETER STYLE GENERAL and PARAMETER STYLE GENERAL WITH NULLS both pass the parameters supplied on the CALL statement. PARAMETER STYLE GENERAL WITH NULLS also passes an additional parameter that includes an array containing a number of elements equal to the number of parameters passed on the CALL statement. A value is returned to each array element to indicate whether or not the corresponding parameter is null.

The DYNAMIC RESULT SETS x option identifies the maximum number of result sets that the procedure can return to the caller, where x represents the number of result sets. This is used when creating stored procedures that incorporate an SQL cursor and a SELECT statement to read data and return the results read to the calling procedure or client application.

55

The SPECIFIC option differentiates procedures with the same name within DB2. A schema or library name can be specified with this option.

The DETERMINISTIC/NON DETERMINISTIC options identify whether or not a procedure called with the same parameter values will return the same results. A DETERMINISTIC procedure may return different results even when parameter values are the same. But a NON DETERMINISTIC procedure will return the same results when the same parameter values are supplied.

The CONTAINS SQL, MODIFIES SQL DATA, NO SQL, and READS SQL DATA options are used to define what type of SQL statements will be executed within the procedure being defined. The CONTAINS SQL option identifies that the procedure being created uses SQL statements. The statements used, however, do not read or update SQL data. The MODIFIES SQL DATA option identifies that our procedure may read and update data. The NO SQL option identifies that the stored procedure does not execute any SQL statements. The READS SQL DATA option is used to define that the procedure can execute SQL statements that read data.

The CALLED ON NULL INPUT option identifies that the procedure is to be executed even if all of the parameters supplied are null. The stored procedure itself must deal with the null conditions internally.

The OLD SAVEPOINT LEVEL and NEW SAVEPOINT LEVEL options define whether or not the procedure will generate a new transaction save point.

Finally, the COMMIT ON RETURN YES/NO options identify whether database transactions should be committed on completion of the procedure.

Now you understand the CREATE PROCEDURE statement, but the CREATE PROCEDURE statement is only a single piece of the stored procedure puzzle. To create SQL stored procedures, you also have to understand the SQL procedure language.

Procedure Language

The elements of SQL used most often within stored procedures look somewhat similar to elements of other programming languages. SQL contains a set of statements used to control the flow of a procedure.

The CALL statement executes a stored procedure. Below is an example of using the CALL statement to call a stored procedure with three parameters.

```
CALL MyProc(PARM1, PARM2, PARM3)
```

The CASE statement in SQL serves multiple purposes. It can be used in the same way it's used in other languages, like RPG—that is, to conditionally execute blocks of code. In this circumstance, there are two options for the coding method used. The first option can be used when each condition associated with the CASE statement is based on the same field. In this circumstance, the statement format would be as follows:

```
CASE fieldname
WHEN comparison_value 1
THEN
     Conditional code;
WHEN comparison value 2
THEN
     Conditional code;
ELSE
     Catch all code;
END CASE
```

The second option is to define the full conditional expression at the WHEN operator. This is useful if each condition is not based on the same field or if the conditional expression is more complex than simply A=B. Using this method, CASE is coded as shown here:

```
CASE
WHEN A=B AND C=0
THEN
     Conditional code;
WHEN A<B OR B>C
THEN
```

57

```
        Conditional code;
ELSE
        Catch all code;
END CASE
```

This example illustrates a CASE group using multiple conditions, including comparisons for "less than" and "greater than" conditions.

In each of these examples, the ELSE statement allows us to code portions of the code to be used as a catch-all.

The FOR statement allows us to execute a segment of code for each row in a defined source table. The code segment below illustrates the use of a FOR group.

```
DECLARE AMT DECIMAL(15,5)
FOR x AS
    Csr1 CURSOR FOR
    SELECT * FROM DETAIL
      DO
      SET AMT=PRICE * QTY;
      UPDATE HEADER SET AMTVAL = AMT WHERE HEADER.ITEM =
      DETAIL.ITEM;
END FOR;
```

This example executes our grouping for each row in the table DETAIL. When each row is read, the value for the fields PRICE and QTY in the DETAIL table are multiplied and stored in local variable AMT. This field is then used to update the field AMTVAL in the table HEADER, based on a matching value for the field ITEM from both tables.

The GET DIAGNOSTICS statement allows us to get various pieces of information related to the last statement executed. The information that can be retrieved includes things like the ROW_COUNT value, which identifies the number of rows returned or affected by an SQL SELECT or UPDATE statement. The statement below illustrates this.

```
DECLARE ROWCT INTEGER;
UPDATE MYTABLE SET FIELD1 = FIELD1 * 1.05
      WHERE UPDFLG = 'Y';
GET DIAGNOSTIC ROWCT = ROW_COUNT;
```

After this code is executed, ROWCT will contain the number of records in the UPDATE statement.

For additional information on the values available and their uses, see the *DB2 UDB for iSeries SQL Reference*.

The SQL GOTO statement is another example of a statement that functions similarly to its counterpart in most other programming languages. This statement transfers program control to the statement identified by the supplied label. The label itself is defined at the beginning of the desired line of code and is followed by a colon (:). The code below illustrates the use of the GOTO statement.

```
BEGIN
DECLARE RETCODE INTEGER DEFAULT 0;
DECLARE ROWCNT INTEGER;
UPDATE MYTABLE SET FLDVAL=1 WHERE FLDUPD='Y';
GET DIAGNOSTIC RETCODE = RETURN_STATUS;
IF RETCODE <> 0 THEN
    GOTO exitcd;
END IF;
GET DIAGNOSTIC ROWCNT = ROW_COUNT;
Exitcd:
END;
```

This example once again makes use of the GET DIAGNOSTIC statement to retrieve the return status for the UPDATE statement. If the value of RETCDE is not 0, procedure control is sent to the Exitcd: label.

In SQL, the IF statement is used much the same way an IF is used in any programming language: to execute a group of statements based on defined conditions. An IF group can also include the modifiers ELSEIF and ELSE to define alternate segments of code when the original condition is not met. ELSEIF allows us to define an alternate condition to the condition originally defined on the IF statement, while ELSE is used as a catch-all. An IF group ends with the END IF statement. Below is a sample IF statement.

```
IF Val1 = 'A' THEN
    Val2 = 12;
ELSEIF Val1='B' AND Val3='X' THEN
    Val2 = 24;
ELSE
    Val2=6;
END IF;
```

Note that each statement ends with the semicolon (;) character. This allows a single SQL statement to span multiple lines. This sample code assigns a value to the field Val2 based on a set of possible conditions.

The LOOP statement performs a similar function to the FOR statement. It causes a group of statements to be executed repeatedly until a command causes the program to exit the loop. The END LOOP statement defines the end of the LOOP group.

The ITERATE statement performs a similar function to GOTO in that it redirects program control to another statement. In this case, however, it causes this control to be returned to the top of the current LOOP grouping. This statement is used only within a LOOP.

The LEAVE statement is used to exit a LOOP by passing control to the first statement after the END LOOP statement. Below is a sample LOOP that illustrates the use of each of these statements.

```
DECLARE CUSNAM CHAR(35);
DECLARE CUSAD1 CHAR(35);
DECLARE CUSAD2 CHAR(35);
DECLARE CUSCTY CHAR(20);
DECLARE CUSSTE CHAR(2);
DECLARE CUSZIP CHAR(10);
DECLARE NOT_FOUND CONDITION FOR SQLSTATE '02000';
DECLARE ErrCode CHAR(1) DEFAULT '0';

DECLARE CSR1 FOR
SELECT CNAME, CADD1, CADD2, CCITY, CSTTE, CZIPC FROM CUSTOMERS;

DECLARE CONTINUE HANDLER FOR NOT_FOUND SET ErrCode = '1';

OPEN CSR1;
Str_loop: LOOP
```

```
FETCH CSR1 INTO CUSNAM, CUSAD1, CUSAD2, CUSSTE, CUSZIP;
IF ErrCode='1' THEN
    LEAVE Str_loop;
ELSEIF CUSSTE <> 'PA' THEN
    ITERATE Str_loop;
END IF;
END LOOP
```

This example prepares an SQL statement using the cursor CSR1. This cursor is then opened and used to fetch records from the file CUSTOMERS. An exception handler is created using DECLARE for a "records not found" condition. When an exception occurs, the value of the field ErrCode is set to '1'. This value is used with an IF statement to control the execution of the LEAVE statement. If that condition does not occur, the value of CUSSTE is used with an ELSEIF statement to compare CUSSTE to 'PA' and conditionally send control to the next iteration of the loop based on that condition.

The REPEAT statement is similar to LOOP in that it repeatedly performs a set of statements. The difference is that REPEAT continues looping until the condition defined on the UNTIL modifier evaluates to true. The sample code below uses the REPEAT condition for end-of-file conditioning.

```
DECLARE CUSNAM CHAR(35);
DECLARE CUSAD1 CHAR(35);
DECLARE CUSAD2 CHAR(35);
DECLARE CUSCTY CHAR(20);
DECLARE CUSSTE CHAR(2);
DECLARE CUSZIP CHAR(10);
DECLARE NOT_FOUND CONDITION FOR SQLSTATE '02000';
DECLARE EOF_COND CHAR(1) DEFAULT '0';

DECLARE CSR1 FOR
SELECT CNAME, CADD1, CADD2, CCITY, CSTTE, CZIPC FROM CUSTOMERS;
DECLARE CONTINUE HANDLER FOR NOT_FOUND SET EOF_COND = '1' ;

OPEN CSR1;
Rpt: REPEAT
FETCH CSR1 INTO CUSNAM, CUSAD1, CUSAD2, CUSSTE, CUSZIP;
INSERT INTO CPYFILE VALUES(CUSNAM,CUSAD1,CUSAD2,CUSSTE,CUSZIP);
UNTIL EOF_COND = '1'
END REPEAT Rpt;
END LOOP
```

As you can see, this example makes use of the same NOT_FOUND handler to determine when our data set is at end of file. The FETCH and INSERT statements will continue to execute until our end-of-file condition occurs.

The SIGNAL and RESIGNAL statements are used for triggering and controlling SQL error conditions. SIGNAL initiates a defined SQLSTATE, while RESIGNAL is used within a continue handler to redefine the existing SQLSTATE. In each of these cases, there is a set of values that can be defined in addition to the SQLSTATE value. Both of these statements are used in the following syntax.

```
SIGNAL/RESIGNAL SQLSTATE string_value / condition_value
    SET signal-var = value
```

When using either statement, the value for the SQLSTATE can be specified two ways. The first way is to use the reserved word SQLSTATE followed by a five-character string value in which the first two positions are the class and the last three are the subclass. Below is an example of signaling a record-not-found condition using this method.

```
SIGNAL SQLSTATE '02000' SET MESSAGE_TEXT = 'RECORD NOT FOUND';
```

The other option is to use a previously declared CONDITION value. The statements below perform the same task shown in the previous example, but we're using a condition value here.

```
DECLARE NOT_FOUND CONDITION FOR SQLSTATE '02000';
SIGNAL NOT_FOUND SET MESSAGE_TEXT = 'RECORD NOT FOUND - CONDITION';
```

Both of these examples use the SET modifier to define a message text value to go with our message.

The SIGNAL and RESIGNAL statements both support 11 informational values. Table 3.1 contains a list of these values along with a description of their use.

Table 3.1: SIGNAL/RESIGNAL Informational Values

Informational Value	Description
CATALOG_NAME	Identifies the name of the database from which the error condition was generated
CLASS_ORIGIN	Defines a string containing source information related to the class portion of the SQLSTATE
COLUMN_NAME	Identifies the column related to the signaled error
CONSTRAINT_CATALOG	Identifies a database containing a constraint related to the defined error
CONSTRAINT_NAME	Defines a string containing the name of the constraint related to the SQLSTATE
CONSTRAINT_SCHEMA	Defines the schema or library containing a constraint related to the error
CURSOR_NAME	Defines a string containing the name of a cursor related to the error that was signaled
MESSAGE_TEXT	Defines a string containing message text related to the error generated
SCHEMA_NAME	Defines the name of a schema related to the SQLSTATE condition
SUBCLASS_ORIGIN	Defines a string containing source information related to the subclass portion of the SQLSTATE
TABLE_NAME	Identifies the source of a schema related to the SQLSTATE condition

When used with the SET operator, these values allow us to further define the error being triggered. While the SIGNAL statement can be used to trigger an error at any point within a procedure, RESIGNAL is used to override an error condition from within an error handler routine.

The RETURN statement is used to exit a stored procedure. A single-integer parameter, which is used as a status value, can be included on the RETURN statement. Below is an example of using the RETURN statement within an SQL procedure.

```
DECLARE NOT_FOUND CONDITION FOR SQLSTATE '02000';
DECLARE EOF_COND INT(10) DEFAULT 0;

BEGIN
DECLARE CSR1 FOR
SELECT CNAME, CADD1, CADD2, CCITY, CSTTE, CZIPC FROM CUSTOMERS;
DECLARE CONTINUE HANDLER FOR NOT_FOUND
SET EOF_COND = -300;

OPEN CSR1;
FETCH CSR1 INTO CUSNAM, CUSAD1, CUSAD2, CUSSTE, CUSZIP;
RETURN EOF_COND;
END;
```

This statement uses a RETURN statement to return an error code (-300) when the required record is not found. The statement returns 0 when a record is found.

The WHILE statement executes a series of statements repeatedly as long as a defined condition is satisfied. Below is a sample of the syntax the WHILE statement uses.

```
DECLARE NAME CHAR(30);
DECLARE NOT_FOUND CONDITION FOR SQLSTATE '02000';
DECLARE EOF_COND INT(10) DEFAULT 0;

BEGIN
DECLARE CSR1 FOR
SELECT CNAME, CADD1, CADD2, CCITY, CSTTE, CZIPC FROM CUSTOMERS;
DECLARE CONTINUE HANDLER FOR NOT_FOUND
SET EOF_COND = -300;

OPEN CSR1;
WHILE EOF_COND = 0 DO
     FETCH CSR1 INTO CUSNAM, CUSAD1, CUSAD2, CUSSTE, CUSZIP;
     SET NAME=CUSNAM;
END WHILE;
END;
```

This statement will continue to execute the FETCH statements as long as the EOF_COND variable is 0. When an end-of-file condition occurs, the value of EOF_COND will be modified by our continue handler and will cause the WHILE condition to end.

Sample Procedures

Let's examine some simple stored procedures that illustrate how to perform common programming tasks from within a stored procedure.

Simple SQL Stored Procedure

The first example we'll explore is a procedure that accepts two parameters, ITEM and CUST. These parameters represent an item number and a customer number and are used within the procedure to build a temporary summary file containing data from multiple tables. Figure 3.1 below contains the source for this procedure.

```
CREATE PROCEDURE QGPL.BLDSUMFILE (
    IN ITEM VARCHAR(255) ,
    IN CUSN VARCHAR(255) )
    LANGUAGE SQL
    SPECIFIC QGPL.BLDSUMFILE
    NOT DETERMINISTIC
    MODIFIES SQL DATA
    CALLED ON NULL INPUT

BEGIN
    DECLARE ITDESC VARCHAR ( 255 ) ;
    DECLARE CUSNAM VARCHAR ( 255 ) ;
    DECLARE SAYR INT ;
    DECLARE SAPR INT ;
    DECLARE ENDOFFILE INT ;
    DECLARE SQTY DEC ( 15 , 5 ) ;
    DECLARE SDOL DEC ( 15 , 5 ) ;
    DECLARE CSR1 DYNAMIC SCROLL CURSOR FOR
            SELECT SAYRSL , SAPRSL, SUM(SQTYSL),SUM(SDOLSL)
            FROM SALES
            WHERE CUSNSL = TRIM(VARCHAR(CUSN,128)) AND
                ITEMSL = TRIM(VARCHAR(ITEM,128))
            GROUP BY SAYRSL , SAPRSL;

    DECLARE CONTINUE HANDLER FOR NOT FOUND SET ENDOFFILE = 1 ;

    CREATE TABLE QTEMP.SUMDATA (ITEMSM CHAR(15),
            DESCSM CHAR(36),CUSNSM CHAR(8),CNAMSM CHAR(36),
            SAYRSM BIGINT,SAPRSM INT,SQTYSM DECIMAL(15,2) ,
            SDOLSM DECIMAL(15,2));
```

Figure 3.1: This example illustrates a simple stored procedure (part 1 of 2).

65

```
        SELECT DESCIT INTO ITDESC FROM ITEMMSTR
               WHERE ITEMIT = TRIM ( VARCHAR ( ITEM , 128 ) );
        SELECT NAMECS INTO CUSNAM FROM CUSTMAST
               WHERE CUSNCS = TRIM ( VARCHAR ( ITEM , 128 ) );

        OPEN CSR1;
        SET ENDOFFILE = 0;

        WHILE ENDOFFILE <> 1 DO
        FETCH NEXT FROM CSR1 INTO SAYR , SAPR , SQTY , SDOL ;
         INSERT INTO QTEMP.SUMDATA VALUES(ITEM,ITDESC,CUSN,
               CUSNAM,SAYR,SAPR,SQTY, SDOL);
        END WHILE;

        CLOSE CSR1 ;
  END   ;
```

Figure 3.1: This example illustrates a simple stored procedure (part 2 of 2).

This procedure can be entered and executed through the iSeries Navigator SQL script plug-in or by placing this code in a source member and executing the SQL statements using the RUNSQLSTM command as shown here:

```
RUNSQLSTM SRCFILE(MYLIB/QSQLSRC) SRCMBR(GETQTY)
```

This procedure is defined as an SQL language procedure that is not deterministic, meaning that if it's called multiple times with the same input parameters, it will return the same data. We begin by declaring the local variables used within the procedure. Next, we define an SQL cursor, which is used to read and summarize data from a sales file. We also declare an exit handler to control program execution when a NOT FOUND (or in this case, end of file) condition occurs. In this case, we change the value of the variable ENDOFFILE to 1. This variable is used in the same way that an end-of-file indicator is used in an RPG program. Next, our procedure creates the temporary table that will contain our summary data. Then, our procedure reads required data from the ITEMMAST and CUSTMAST tables. Note that the SELECT INTO statement is used to retrieve a value from a table. This method can be used only when the result of the SELECT statement is a single record. Once these values have been read, our procedure opens the SQL cursor defined earlier and uses a FETCH statement embedded within a WHILE DO group to read each record within the cursor and output the combined data into the table QTEMP.SUMDATA. When created, this procedure can be executed from a variety of applications. We can, for example, execute this procedure from within another SQL procedure by using the CALL statement as shown below.

```
CREATE PROCEDURE SOMEPROC()
LANGUAGE SQL BEGIN
...
    CALL QGPL.BLDSUMFILE('ABCDEF','123456');
...
END;
```

In addition to using this procedure from within an SQL procedure, we can also call this procedure from within an RPG program by using embedded SQL. The ILE RPG program shown in Figure 3.2 illustrates this.

```
 *_____
 *
 * Program: SQL001LE Function: Example of calling a stored procedure
 *                            from within an ILE RPG program using

 *                            embedded SQL statements.
 *
 * Create Command  CRTSQLRPGI PGM(lib/SQL001LE)
 *                            SRCFILE(lib/QRPGLESRC)
 *                            SRCMBR(SQL001LE)
 *_____
FSQL001FM    CF    E            WORKSTN
C                        EXFMT   SQL001F1
C                        IF      *INKC=*OFF
C/EXEC SQL
C+ CALL QGPL.BLDSUMFILE(:WSITEM, :WSCUST)
C/END-EXEC
C       'File created'DSPLY
C                        EndIf
C                        Eval    *INLR=*ON
C                        Return
```

Figure 3.2: This RPG program is used to call a stored procedure.

When this program is called, a screen is displayed that prompts the user for an item and a customer number. The embedded SQL CALL statement, denoted by the EXEC SQL and END-EXEC compiler directives, is then used to execute the BLDSUMFILE stored procedure. Once the stored procedure completes execution, a message is returned indicating that the summary file has been built, but your application could easily continue to process using the summary file that was generated.

This example helps to illustrate how you might perform a task that would otherwise be accomplished within an RPG program in a stored procedure.

SQL stored procedures also offer a great deal of portability, simply because you can use embedded SQL to call SQL procedures from within a variety of languages or even from a Windows client application using ADO or JDBC calls. When speaking of portability, it's important to remember that we create SQL procedures using programs written in languages other than SQL. As examined earlier, these external stored procedures allow us to take existing applications and retool them for use as SQL stored procedures, thereby making them accessible to SQL language applications.

ILE RPG External Stored Procedure

When declaring an external stored procedure, we still need to use the CREATE PROCEDURE function to create the stored procedure. The primary difference will be the LANGUAGE parameter. When defining a stored procedure named GetQty that works with an existing ILE RPG program, PRG001LE, which accepts two input parameters, ITEM and CUST, and outputs a third parameter, QTY, we would use the CREATE PROCEDURE statement shown in Figure 3.3.

```
CREATE PROCEDURE GetQty (IN ITEM CHAR(15), IN CUST CHAR(8),
       OUT QTY DECIMAL(15,5))
EXTERNAL NAME MYLIB.PRG001LE
LANGUAGE RPGLE
PARAMETER STYLE GENERAL
```

Figure 3.3: This example creates a stored procedure using an ILE RPG program.

When this statement is executed, a new entry is made into the SYSPROCS view in the QSYS2 library. The result is that the ILE RPG program is now callable from within SQL because an SQL procedure definition exists for the program. This means that you can call this procedure from an ADO or JDBC client application. With that idea in mind, I'd like to examine a few stored procedures that can be used to execute commands from a remote client application.

CL External Stored Procedure

The first example of a stored procedure that can be called from a remote client application one is based on the CL program shown in Figure 3.4.

```
/*------------------------------------------------------------------*/
/*                                                                  */
/* PROGRAM NAME: GETSYSVAL   RETURN THE VALUE OF THE DEFINED SYSTEM VALUE */
/*                                                                  */
/* CREATE COMMAND: CRTCLPGM PGM(XXX/GETSYSVAL)                      */
/*                          SRCFILE(XXX/QCLSRC)                     */
/*                                                                  */
/*------------------------------------------------------------------*/
          PGM        PARM(&SYSVALIN &VALOUT)

          DCL        VAR(&SYSVALIN) TYPE(*CHAR) LEN(10)

          DCL        VAR(&VALOUT) TYPE(*CHAR) LEN(30)

          RTVSYSVAL  SYSVAL(&SYSVALIN) RTNVAR(&VALOUT)
          MONMSG     MSGID(CPF0001) EXEC(CHGVAR VAR(&VALOUT) +
                     VALUE('*SYSVAL=' || &SYSVALIN *TCAT ' +
                     INVALID*'))

          ENDPGM
```

Figure 3.4: This CL program is used to retrieve system values.

This CL program has two parameters; one is used as an input parameter to provide the name of a system value, and other is used as an output parameter to return the value for the supplied system value. This CL program is created using the CRTCLPGM command shown here:

```
CRTCLPGM PGM(XXX/GETSYSVAL) SRCFILE(XXX/QCLSRC)
```

Here, *xxx* represents the library containing the CL source.

To convert the compiled program data into a stored procedure, we would again use the CREATE PROCEDURE statement. Figure 3.5 shows the code required to create a procedure using our CL program.

```
CREATE PROCEDURE GETSYSVAL(IN SYSVAL CHAR ( 10),
OUT VALOUT CHAR (30))
LANGUAGE CL
NOT DETERMINISTIC
CONTAINS SQL
EXTERNAL NAME MYLIB.GETSYSVAL
PARAMETER STYLE GENERAL
```

Figure 3.5: This statement creates our stored procedure.

When executed, this statement creates the stored procedure representation of our GetSysVal CL program. This procedure can be used to retrieve an iSeries system value from a client application via an ADO or a JDBC connection. As an example of how this works, Figure 3.6 shows sample source for an Active Server Page (ASP), which uses an ADO connection to retrieve a system value from the iSeries.

```
<HTML>
<%

Set objConn = Server.CreateObject("ADODB.Connection")
Set objCmd = Server.CreateObject("ADODB.Command")
objConn.Open  "DRIVER=Client Access ODBC Driver (32-bit); " & _
        "UID=user; PWD=secret; System=MYAS400; TRANSLATE=1;"

objCmd.ActiveCOnnection = objConn

objCmd.CommandText = "{CALL MFAUST.GETSYSVAL (?, ?)}"
objCmd.Parameters.Refresh
objCmd.Parameters(0) = "QTIME       "
objCmd.Execute

Response.Write objCmd.Parameters(0) & "=" & objCmd.Parameters(1)
%>
</HTML>
```

Figure 3.6: This ASP application uses our newly created GetSysVal procedure.

If this file is saved on an ASP-compatible Web server and loaded in a Web browser, the result is that the value of the iSeries system value QTIME is displayed. Figure 3.7 shows what this output looks like.

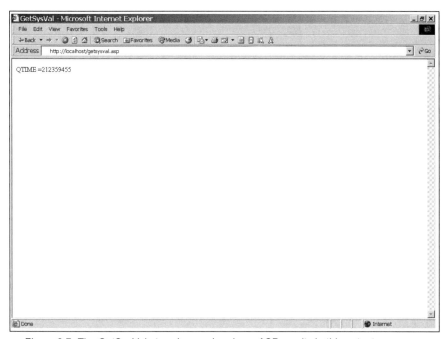

Figure 3.7: The GetSysVal stored procedure in an ASP results in this output.

This example helps to illustrate how the use of stored procedures can be extended far beyond just use on the iSeries. As you can see, this gives us the ability to execute an iSeries program from a non-iSeries client application, complete with input and output parameters. This universal use concept is greatly extended by the ability to use applications written in other iSeries languages, such as RPG or even CL, as is the case with this example.

DeleteDups Stored Procedure

Stored procedures can also help to simplify what would otherwise be complicated tasks. One example of this is a stored procedure that handles locating and removing duplicate records from a physical file, a process that would normally require writing a program or manually deleting records using a utility like DFU. Figure 3.8 contains the source for the DeleteDups stored procedure.

```
-- DELETE DUPLICATE RECORDS FILE A SPECIFIED TABLE
--
-- PRIOR TO EXECUTING EXISTING PROCEDURE MUST BE DELETED
-- USING THE STATEMENT; DROP PROCEDURE QGPL.DELETEDUPS
--
CREATE PROCEDURE QGPL.DELETEDUPS(IN @LIB VARCHAR(20),
                                 IN @FILE VARCHAR(20))
LANGUAGE SQL
SPECIFIC QGPL.DELETEDUPS
NOT DETERMINISTIC
MODIFIES SQL DATA
BEGIN
      DECLARE STMT VARCHAR ( 8000 ) ;   -- SQL STATEMENT
      DECLARE FLDS VARCHAR ( 2000 ) ;   -- FIELDS
      DECLARE WHR VARCHAR ( 2000 ) ;    -- WHR CLAUSE
      DECLARE ROWCNT DECIMAL(10, 0) ;   -- ROW COUNT
      DECLARE COL DECIMAL(10, 0) ;       -- COLUMN
      DECLARE COLNM VARCHAR (20) ;       -- COLUMN
      DECLARE  CRSR CURSOR FOR SELECT COLUMN_NAME FROM QSYS2.SYSCOLUMNS
              WHERE TABLE_NAME = @FILE AND TABLE_SCHEMA = @LIB;
      DECLARE CSR2 CURSOR FOR SQLSTMT;

      OPEN CRSR;
      SET ROWCNT = (SELECT COUNT(*) FROM QSYS2.SYSCOLUMNS
              WHERE TABLE_NAME = @FILE AND TABLE_SCHEMA = @LIB);
      SET FLDS = ' ';
      SET WHR = ' ';
      SET COL = 0;
      WHILE COL < ROWCNT DO
        SET COL=COL + 1;
        FETCH NEXT FROM CRSR INTO COLNM;
        SET FLDS = TRIM(FLDS) || COLNM;

        SET WHR = TRIM(WHR) || ' X.' || COLNM || ' = Y.' || COLNM;
        IF COL < ROWCNT THEN
          SET FLDS = TRIM(FLDS) || ', ';
          SET WHR = TRIM(WHR) || ' AND ';
        END IF;
      END WHILE;
      SET STMT = 'DELETE FROM ' || @LIB || '.' ||@FILE|| ' AS X WHERE RRN(X)<>'
              || '(SELECT MAX(RRN(Y)) AS GOODREC ' ||
              ' FROM ' || @LIB || '.' || @FILE || ' AS Y WHERE ' || WHR ||
              ' GROUP BY ' || TRIM(FLDS) || ' HAVING COUNT(*)>1)';
      PREPARE SQLSTMT FROM STMT;
      EXECUTE SQLSTMT;
END;
```

Figure 3.8: This stored procedure deletes duplicate records.

This procedure accepts input parameters containing the library and file names for the file that requires duplicate record deletion. Note that the MODIFY SQL DATA operator is specified to identify that our procedure is going to change data using SQL statements. The body of the stored procedure begins by declaring the variables used within the procedure. These include three variables that will be used to dynamically build the SQL DELETE statement to remove the duplicate records. The next three variables identify the columns within the table to be updated. Next, an SQL cursor is defined. This cursor will be used to read the column names for the required file from the SYSCOLUMNS system view, which contains column-level data for each table on the system. The ROWCNT variable identifies the number of columns in the table. This value is compared to the COL variable to determine when all columns have been processed. The column names for the file name supplied to the procedure are added to the character variables FLDS and WHR. These two variables are used later to build the DELETE statement, which will handle the duplicate record removal. Once all of the columns have been read, the procedure builds this DELETE statement in the variable STMT. The deletion is accomplished by using a subquery based on the FLDS and WHR variables along with the @LIB and @FILE variables, which contain the library and file names. The result of this subquery contains the highest relative record number for each group of duplicate records. Record matching is done in the subquery's WHERE clause. Assuming we had a file named MYFILE in the library MYLIB with fields named A, B, and C, the following DELETE statement would be generated by this part of the procedure.

```
DELETE FROM MYLIB.MYFILE AS X WHERE RRN(X) <>
      (SELECT MAX(RRN(Y)) AS GOODREC MYLIB.MYFILE AS Y
      WHERE X.A = Y.A AND X.B = Y.B AND X.C = Y.C
      GROUP BY A,B,C HAVING COUNT(*)>1)
```

Note that the built-in function MAX is used with the built-in function RRN to allow us to determine the most recently created duplicate record in each group. The subquery selects the record number value for records with more than one record with identical values. This is determined using the HAVING clause, which allows us to define criteria on a group by using the GROUP BY clause. The records in question are selected only when the values for fields A, B, and C match the current record in the DELETE statement. Once this stored procedure has been created, we can execute it from the interactive SQL command line using the statement shown below.

```
CALL QGPL.DELETEDUPS('MYLIB', 'MYFILE')
```

If the procedure is called successfully, the message "CALL statement complete" is returned. If an error occurs, an error message is returned.

This example illustrates a common type of stored procedure that is used for database maintenance purposes.

Crosstab Stored Procedure

The next stored procedure we're going to examine is written using SQL procedure language and allows us to emulate a Microsoft Access crosstab query. This functionality summarizes data based on two elements within a table and creates a two-dimensional view of that data within an SQL table. This can be illustrated using the sample data shown in Table 3.2 below.

Table 3.2: Crosstab Query Sample Data		
CUSNO	**TRNPER**	**TRNQTY**
0123444	200409	24
0123444	200409	32
0123444	200410	47
0123444	200501	30
0987654	200409	125
0987654	200410	115
0987654	200410	120
0987654	200412	114
0456987	200409	75
0456987	200410	80
0456987	200411	55
0456987	200501	67
0456987	200501	72

This example contains three columns that will be used by our stored procedure. These columns contain a customer number (CUSNO), a transaction period (TRN-PER) in the yyyymm format, and a transaction quantity (TRNQTY). When executing a crosstab on this data, we can summarize each customer by period and display the data in a format that is more "user-friendly." Table 3.3 shows the result of a crosstab using the transaction period for the column, the customer number for the row, and the transaction quantity for the crosstab value.

Table 3.3: Crosstab Result

CUSNO	200409	200410	200411	200412	200501
0123444	56	47			30
0987654	125	235		114	
0456987	75	80	55		139

The resulting crosstab displays one column for each distinct value found in the field TRNPER and summarizes the values from the field TRNQTY for each different CUSNO value. As you can see, the resulting data is a much more concise view of the record set.

Now that I've explained the concept, let's take a look at the stored procedure that will perform this function. Figure 3.9 contains the source for the stored procedure CROSSTAB.

```
CREATE PROCEDURE QGPL.CROSSTAB (

IN TBLNAME VARCHAR(255) ,
IN COLFLDNM VARCHAR(255) ,
IN ROWFLDNM VARCHAR(255) ,
IN VALUEFLD VARCHAR(255) )
DYNAMIC RESULT SETS 1
LANGUAGE SQL
SPECIFIC QGPL.CROSSTAB
NOT DETERMINISTIC
```

Figure 3.9: This source is used to create the CROSSTAB stored procedure (part 1 of 3).

```
MODIFIES SQL DATA
CALLED ON NULL INPUT
BEGIN
  DECLARE STMT VARCHAR ( 8000 ) ;  -- SQL Statement
  DECLARE RTN VARCHAR ( 255 ) ;   -- RETURN Values
  DECLARE COLNM VARCHAR ( 255 ) ;   -- Current column name
  DECLARE COL# SMALLINT ;   -- Column Number
  DECLARE COLCNT SMALLINT ;   -- Column Count
  DECLARE WIDECOL INTEGER ;   -- the widest column lengthCON
  DECLARE SQLSTTE CHAR ( 5 ) DEFAULT '00000' ;
  DECLARE MAXCOLS BIGINT ;
  DECLARE ROW_COUNT INT ;
  DECLARE I INT ;
  DECLARE MAXCOLNMLN SMALLINT ;
  DECLARE MAXSTMLEN SMALLINT ;
  DECLARE ERRSEV INT ;
  DECLARE SQLSTCOND CONDITION FOR SQLSTATE '02000' ;
  DECLARE X_TAB CURSOR FOR
    SELECT COLFLD FROM QTEMP . CROSSCOL
    ORDER BY COLFLD ;
  DECLARE CSR2 CURSOR WITH RETURN FOR SQLSTMT ;

  SET MAXCOLS = 255 ;
  SET MAXSTMLEN = 8000 ;
  SET MAXCOLNMLN = 128 ;
  SET ERRSEV = 11 ;

  IF TBLNAME IS NULL OR COLFLDNM IS NULL
  OR ROWFLDNM IS NULL OR VALUEFLD IS NULL THEN
    SIGNAL SQLSTATE '02000' SET MESSAGE_TEXT =
    'Required Parameter not Found' ;
    RETURN ROW_COUNT ;
  END IF ;

  CREATE TABLE QTEMP.CROSSCOL ( COLFLD VARCHAR ( 255 ) ) ;
  CREATE TABLE QTEMP.SQLFILE ( SQLSTM VARCHAR ( 1024 ) ) ;

  SET STMT = ' INSERT INTO QTEMP.CROSSCOL SELECT DISTINCT '
    || COLFLDNM || ' FROM ' || TBLNAME ;
  PREPARE SQLSTMT FROM STMT ;
  EXECUTE SQLSTMT ;
  SELECT COUNT( * ) INTO COLCNT FROM QTEMP.CROSSCOL ;

  IF COLCNT > MAXCOLS THEN
    SIGNAL SQLSTATE '02000' SET MESSAGE_TEXT =
    'Exceeded maximum number of columns in Cross-tab' ;
    RETURN 0 ;
```

Figure 3.9: This source is used to create the CROSSTAB stored procedure (part 2 of 3).

```
    ELSEIF COLCNT = 0 THEN
      SIGNAL SQLSTATE '02000' SET MESSAGE_TEXT =
          No Data Returned' ;
    RETURN 0 ;
    ELSE
      SELECT INT(MAX(LENGTH(VARCHAR(COLFLD, 129))))
          INTO WIDECOL FROM QTEMP . CROSSCOL ;
    END IF ;

    SET STMT = '' ;
    SET STMT = 'SELECT IFNULL(VARCHAR( ' || ROWFLDNM
      || ', 255),''Undefined'') As '
      || ROWFLDNM || ', ' ;

    OPEN X_TAB ;

      FETCH NEXT FROM X_TAB INTO COLNM ;
    SET I = 0 ;
    WHILE I < COLCNT DO
      SET I = I + 1 ;
      SET COLNM = IFNULL(COLNM , 'Undefined') ;
      SET VALUEFLD = IFNULL(VALUEFLD , 'Undefined') ;  --
    IF I > 1 THEN
      SET STMT = STMT || ', ' ;
    END IF ;

    SET STMT = STMT || ' SUM(CASE WHEN VARCHAR( ' || COLFLDNM
      || ', 128) = '''
      || COLNM || ''' THEN ' || VALUEFLD || ' ELSE 0 END) AS "' ||
      VARCHAR ( COLNM , 128 ) || '" ' ;


    FETCH NEXT FROM X_TAB INTO COLNM ;

    END WHILE ;

    SET STMT = TRIM(TRIM(STMT) || ' FROM ' || TRIM(
      CHAR(TBLNAME , 128 ) ) ||
        ' GROUP BY ' || TRIM(VARCHAR(ROWFLDNM , 128)) );
    IF LENGTH(STMT) >= MAXSTMLEN THEN
        SIGNAL SQLSTATE '02000' SET MESSAGE_TEXT =
        'Generated SQL Statement Exceeds Maximum length
        of 8000 Characters' ;
        RETURN 0 ;
    END IF ;
    CLOSE X_TAB ;
    PREPARE SQLSTMT FROM STMT ;
    OPEN CSR2 ;
    SET RESULT SETS CURSOR CSR2 ;
END;
```

Figure 3.9: This source is used to create the CROSSTAB stored procedure (part 3 of 3).

77

This stored procedure uses some techniques we've already examined, along with a few we haven't. This procedure begins by declaring the variables used within our application and then declaring a condition handler used to handle end-of-file conditions. Next, we declare an SQL cursor that will be used to read unique column values later. We then define some static values used within our procedure prior to performing an edit check to ensure that all required parameters have a supplied value. Next, a CREATE TABLE statement is executed to build the table that will contain a list of unique values for the field defined as our crosstab column. Values are inserted into this table using an SQL statement prepared from a supplied string value. This prepared statement is then executed, which in turn builds the list of required column values. Then, our procedure reads through each of these column values and uses the values read in to create a custom column within a dynamically built SQL statement. The result of this statement will act as the result set returned by our procedure. Each column is built using the CASE operator, which allows us to conditionally identify the value for a column. The statement below illustrates using CASE to split data into two columns based on a value from a different column.

```
SELECT ITEM, SUM(CASE WHEN ITYEAR = 2004 THEN ITQTY ELSE 0 END) AS
QTY_2004,
        SUM(CASE WHEN ITYEAR = 2005 THEN ITQTY ELSE 0 END) AS QTY_2005
FROM ITEMQTY WHERE YEAR>=2004
GROUP BY ITEM
```

The CASE operator in this example will return the value of the field ITQTY if the condition shown results to true; otherwise, a value of 0 is returned. When this statement is executed, three columns will be returned: ITEM, QTY_2004, and QTY_2005.

The values are summarized by item number, resulting in a single record for each item showing the total ITQTY for the two years displayed, each in its own column. Our CROSSTAB stored procedure automates this process, allowing the user to supply the source table name, the column field name, the row field name, and the name of the field containing the value to be summarized.

The code shown in Figure 3.10 illustrates how to call this stored procedure from a Visual Basic for Applications (VBA) application. This code can be used within Microsoft Office applications like Access or Excel.

```
Dim conn As New ADODB.Connection
Dim rs As New ADODB.Recordset
Dim cmd As New ADODB.Command

conn.Open "Provider=IBMDA400;Data Source=192.168.0.3"
stmt = "{CALL CrossTab('QGPL.MYFILE', '''Year'' ||
YEAR','ITEM','SALES')}"


rs.Open stmt, conn
stra = ""
For x = 0 To rs.Fields.Count - 1
stra = stra & " " & rs.Fields(x).Name
Next
Debug.Print stra

Do Until rs.EOF
strb = ""
For x = 0 To rs.Fields.Count - 1
strb = strb & " " & rs.Fields(x).Value
Next
rs.MoveNext
Debug.Print strb
Loop
```

Figure 3.10: This VBA source is used to call our CROSSTAB stored procedure.

When executed, this code snippet connects to our data source using the IBMDA400 OLE DB provider and then calls our stored procedure. The data returned appears as it would if the data source were a regular table. The columns returned by this code look something like Table 3.4.

Table 3.4: Resulting Data Displayed in Crosstab Format

Item	Year 2000	Year 2002	Year 2003	Year 2004
ABC123	40	20	0	0
DEF456	35	35	35	45
HIJ789	40	39	44	0

You'll notice that our column labels are built using the expression '"Year" ||
ITYEAR'. This allows us to combine the string value "Year" with the field value
ITYEAR from our source data file. This makes our resulting column name more
readable and allows us to avoid ending up with a column name that is strictly
numeric.

Stored Procedure Wrap-Up

In this chapter, we've discovered how the ability to create stored procedures
from existing iSeries programs makes it quick and easy to extend the use of the
applications that you've already developed. This can be a great timesaver when
developing client/server applications that are intended to replace existing tasks
on the iSeries. You can replace the front-end portion of batch update applications
with a simple Web page or other client application and, after entries are made,
call a stored procedure version of the batch update program. While the examples
we've explored in this chapter have been distinctly different, they've all shared a
common thread: They've helped to illustrate how easy it is to build and use custom SQL stored procedures with the iSeries DB2 database.

4

Creating User-Defined Functions

Just as SQL allows us to create stored procedures, SQL also allows us to create our own user-defined functions. These functions can be used to perform complex calculations that can be fed into a single field value. The DB2 UDB for iSeries implementation of SQL supports two types of user-defined functions (UDFs). As we examined earlier, scalar functions allow us to return a value used for a single column's value. User-defined functions also allow us to create a function that returns multiple column values in the form of their own table. In this chapter, we'll examine creating both types of user-defined functions.

Language Elements

To create user-defined functions, we'll be using the same SQL procedure language elements that we used to create stored procedures in chapter 3. The big difference is in how functions are created and used. As with stored procedures, user-defined functions can be created using either the SQL procedural language or applications written in many of the other languages supported on the iSeries. This fact, coupled with the fact that we can create table functions and scalar functions, increases the complexity of the CREATE FUNCTION statement. This means that we effectively have four possible types of functions:

- External scalar functions

- External table functions

- SQL scalar functions

- SQL table functions

In addition, we have the ability to create "sourced" functions. Sourced SQL functions are functions that are based on other user-defined functions. These can be used as an alternative method to call an existing function. Let's start out by examining the syntax of the CREATE FUNCTION statement for each of these circumstances.

External Scalar Functions

This type of user-defined SQL function, as with its built-in function counterpart, allows us to return a single value for each row in a table. When used to create an external scalar function, the CREATE FUNCTION statement requires many of the same parameters used to create a stored procedure. Figure 4.1 below shows the syntax used to create a "non-SQL" user-defined function.

```
CREATE FUNCTION function_name (parm1, parm2, etc.)
RETURNS return_variable
EXTERNAL NAME library.program
LANGUAGE language_name
PARAMETER STYLE parameter definition style
```

Figure 4.1: This example illustrates the use of CREATE FUNCTION.

You'll notice that the syntax is fairly similar to that used with the CREATE PROCEDURE function. The RETURNS modifier defines the single value to be returned by the function. The EXTERNAL NAME value allows us to identify the existing program that will be used to perform the function. The LANGUAGE modifier is used, as it was in CREATE PROCEDURE, to define the programming language for the associated EXTERNAL NAME value. The PARAMETER STYLE defines the type of parameter definition that will be returned to the function.

PARAMETER STYLE DB2GENERAL can only be used when the programming language identified on the LANGUAGE parameter is Java. This parameter style defines that the function will have the number of input parameters identified in the function's parameter definitions as well as one output parameter as defined on the RETURN parameter.

PARAMETER STYLE GENERAL is only available when the external program defined on the EXTERNAL NAME parameter is a service program. This parameter style accepts the number of parameters defined in the function's parameter definition and returns the value as defined on the RETURNS modifier.

PARAMETER STYLE GENERAL WITH NULLS is also used only when the external program defined on the EXTERNAL NAME parameter is a service program. This parameter style accepts the number of parameters defined in the function's parameter definition in addition to a variable that contains an array of indicators with a number of elements matching the number of parameters in our function. One other parameter is passed as an indicator variable for the function's RETURN value. The return value itself is defined on the RETURNS modifier.

PARAMETER STYLE JAVA uses a parameter style similar to the Java language parameter structure. The function passes all parameters identified on the function's parameter definition, and the return value is passed back as it is defined on the RETURNS modifier. Needless to say, this parameter style is only applicable when the LANGUAGE parameter is JAVA. The PARAMETER STYLE JAVA and PARAMETER STYLE DB2GENERAL are identical with the exception that PARAMETER STYLE JAVA doesn't support table functions, scratchpads, FINAL CALL functionality, or access to the DBINFO data structure.

You'll notice that these parameter styles are quite similar to those used with the CREATE PROCEDURE statement. While the definition shown in Figure 4.1 is sufficient to define a function, there are additional modifiers available that can be used to give greater definition detail to a function definition.

The SPECIFIC parameter can be used to define a unique name for a function in cases where multiple copies of a function may exist on your system.

The DETERMINISTIC and NON-DETERMINISTIC modifiers are used in exactly the same way they are used within a CREATE PROCEDURE statement. These modifiers identify whether or not successive calls to the same function with the same parameters will return the same result. The value DETERMINIS-TIC identifies that successive calls to the function with the same parameters will return the same result, while NON-DETERMINISTIC defines that successive calls with the same parameter values may not return the same results.

The modifiers CONTAINS SQL, READS SQL DATA, MODIFIES SQL DATA, and NO SQL are each used to define what, if any, type of SQL statements are contained within the function.

The modifiers RETURNS NULL ON NULL INPUT and CALLED ON NULL INPUT define what should happen when the function is called with a null value on a parameter. RETURNS NULL ON NULL INPUT will prevent the function from being called when any parameter is null. In this circumstance, the value returned for the function will also be null. CALLED ON NULL INPUT will allow the function to be executed even if a parameter is null. In this circumstance, the function itself must be able to handle the null value.

The modifiers DBINFO and NO DBINFO define whether or not a data structure should be passed containing additional information about the database containing the function. The DBINFO structure allows you to acquire that additional information about your database and function. Figure 4.2 contains the source for this structure, which can be found in the source file SQLUDF in the source file H in library QSYSINC.

```
SQL_STRUCTURE   sqludf_dbinfo
{
  unsigned short  dbnamelen;                      /* database name length    */
  unsigned char   dbname[SQLUDF_MAX_IDENT_LEN];   /* database name           */
  unsigned short  authidlen;                      /* authorization ID length */
  unsigned char   authid[SQLUDF_MAX_IDENT_LEN];   /* appl authorization ID   */
  union db_cdpg   codepg;                         /* database code page      */
  unsigned short  tbschemalen;                    /* table schema name length*/
  unsigned char   tbschema[SQLUDF_MAX_IDENT_LEN]; /* table schema name       */
  unsigned short  tbnamelen;                      /* table name length       */
  unsigned char   tbname[SQLUDF_MAX_IDENT_LEN];   /* table name              */
  unsigned short  colnamelen;                     /* column name length      */
  unsigned char   colname[SQLUDF_MAX_IDENT_LEN];  /* column name             */
  unsigned char   ver_rel[SQLUDF_SH_IDENT_LEN];
  unsigned char   resd0[2];                       /* alignment               */
  unsigned long   platform;
  unsigned short  numtfcol;                       /* number of entries in    */
                                                  /* the TF column list array*/
                                                  /* (tfcolumn, below)       */

  unsigned char   resd1[38];                      /* Reserved- for expansion */
  unsigned short  *tfcolumn;
  char            *appl_id;                       /* application identifier  */
  unsigned char   resd2[20];                      /* Reserved- for expansion */
}
```

Figure 4.2: This illustrates the data contained in the DBINFO structure.

The EXTERNAL ACTION/NO EXTERNAL ACTION modifiers allow you to define whether or not the external program that carries out the function performs actions other than those required by the function. The SQL optimizer uses this option to decide whether to either invoke the function or simply use cached results each time the function is evoked.

The FENCED and NOT FENCED options identify whether the function runs in its own thread or runs in the same thread that the database manager runs in.

The FINAL CALL/NO FINAL CALL option identifies whether a final call must be made to a function. When this option is used, an additional parameter indicates whether or not the current invocation is the final call.

ALLOW PARALLEL and DISALLOW PARALLEL allow us to define whether or not the function can be run in parallel.

SCRATCHPAD allows you to define an area of memory that is allocated to the function. Optionally, a value can be specified to define the size of the scratchpad area. The NO SCRATCHPAD option identifies that the function doesn't require a scratchpad.

Now that I've explained the syntax required to create an external scalar function, let's examine a useful sample function. Figure 4.3 contains the source for the ILE RPG program EDITCODE. As you might imagine, this function allows us to convert a numeric value into a representation of the number using RPG edit codes. This function is the SQL equivalent of ILE RPG's EDITC function.

```
H DftActGrp(*NO) ActGrp(*Caller) BNDDIR('QC2LE')
 *
 *   Program: EDITCD
 *
 *   Description: Sample program for use as an External Scalar Function words
 *
 *   Compile command: CRTBNDRPG   PGM(mylib/EDITC)
 *                                SRCFILE(mylib/QRPGLESRC)
 *                                SRCRBR(EDITC2)
 *
DEDITCODE         PR
D InVal                          15  5
D EdtCde                          1
D OutVal                         30
DEDITCODE         PI
D InValue                        15  5
D EditCd                          1
D OutValue                       30
DDecimal8         S               8  0
 /Free
   Select;
   When EditCd = '1';
     OutValue = %EditC(InValue: '1');
   When EditCd = '2';
     OutValue = %EditC(InValue: '2');
   When EditCd = '3';
     OutValue = %EditC(InValue: '3');
   When EditCd = '4';
     OutValue = %EditC(InValue: '4');
   When EditCd = 'A';
     OutValue = %EditC(InValue: 'A');
   When EditCd = 'B';
     OutValue = %EditC(InValue: 'B');
   When EditCd = 'C';
     OutValue = %EditC(InValue: 'C');
```

Figure 4.3: This program will be used as an external scalar function (part 1 of 2).

```
  When EditCd = 'D';
   OutValue = %EditC(InValue: 'D');
  When EditCd = 'J';
   OutValue = %EditC(InValue: 'J');
  When EditCd = 'K';
   OutValue = %EditC(InValue: 'K');
  When EdiTCd = 'L';
   OutValue = %EditC(InValue: 'L');
  When EditCd = 'M';
   OutValue = %EditC(InValue: 'M');
  When EditCd = 'N';
   OutValue = %EditC(InValue: 'N');
  When EditCd = 'O';
   OutValue = %EditC(InValue: 'O');
  When EditCd = 'P';
   OutValue = %EditC(InValue: 'P');
  When EditCd = 'Q';
   OutValue = %EditC(InValue: 'Q');
  When EditCd = 'Y';
   Decimal8 = InValue;
   OutValue = %EditC(Decimal8: 'Y');
  When EditCd = 'Z';
   OutValue = %EditC(InValue: 'Z');
  Other;
   OutValue = 'Error: Invalid Edit Code';
  EndSl;
  Return;
 /end-free
```

Figure 4.3: This program will be used as an external scalar function (part 2 of 2).

This function accepts the numeric value to be converted (InValue) and the corresponding edit code (EditCd). The third parameter shown is used to pass the edited value to the caller (OutValue). The function then uses the ILE RPG built-in function %EDITC to edit the supplied numeric value.

The CREATE FUNCTION statement shown in Figure 4.4 is used to create the SQL function definition for this external program.

```
CREATE FUNCTION MYLIB.EDITCODE(@InValue NUMERIC (15 , 5),
                              @EditCd varchar (1))
RETURNS CHAR (30)
LANGUAGE RPGLE
PARAMETER STYLE DB2SQL
EXTERNAL NAME MYLIB.EDITCODE
```

Figure 4.4: This statement builds the SQL interface to our RPG program.

Once executed, our function is accessible from any interface that utilizes an SQL interface. This includes the interactive SQL interface (STRSQL). To test our newly created function, we need to start this interface by going to a command line and typing STRSQL. When the Interactive SQL prompt is displayed, type the following SQL SELECT statement:

```
SELECT MYLIB.EDITCODE(DECIMAL(12145.36, 15, 5), 'B')
  FROM QSYS2.SYSFUNCS
```

This example uses the SYSFUNCS table purely as a "driver" for the rest of the process. In this example, we convert the value for the first parameter to a decimal value to match what is required by the ILE RPG program behind the scenes. When this statement is executed, a string representation of the numeric value is returned in the defined edited format. In this example, the result would be 12,145.36000.

Let's examine one more external scalar function. This time our function will be used to return a state name from a supplied state abbreviation. Figure 4.5 contains the ILE RPG source for this function.

```
H DftActGrp(*NO) ActGrp(*Caller) BNDDIR('QC2LE')
 *
 *   Program: STATENAME
 *
 *   Description: Lookup State Name
 *
 *   Compile command: CRTBNDRPG PGM(mylib/STATENAME)
 *                              SRCFILE(mylib/QRPGLESRC)
 *                              SRCRBR(STATENAME)
 *
DSTATENAME        PR
D StAb                          2
D StNm                         20
DSTATENAME        PI
D StAbbr                        2
D StName                       20
 * State Compile Time Array
D Sttabb          S            2        DIM(50) CTDATA
   PERRCD(1)
D Stnames         S           26        DIM(50) CTDATA
```

Figure 4.5: This program returns a state name from the supplied abbreviation (part 1 of 4).

```
          PERRCD(1)
     D El                S              5 0
       /Free
          El = %LOOKUP(StAbbr: Sttabb);
          If El = 0;
             StName = '* Error';
          Else;
             StName = Stnames(El);
          EndIf;
          Return;
       /End-Free
        *
** State Abbreviation Table
AL
AK
AZ
AR
CA
CO
CT
DE
FL
GA
HI
ID
IL
IN
IA
KS
KY
LA
ME
MD
MA
MI
MN
MS
MO
MT
NE
NV
NH
NJ
NM
NY
NC
ND
OH
```

Figure 4.5: This program returns a state name from the supplied abbreviation (part 2 of 4).

```
OK
OR
PA
RI
SC
SD
TN
TX
UT
VT
VA
WA
WV
WI
WY
** State names table
Alabama
Alaska
Arizona
Arkansas
California
Colorado
Connecticut
Delaware
Florida
Georgia
Hawaii
Idaho
Illinois
Indiana
Iowa
Kansas
Kentucky
Louisiana
Maine
Maryland
Massachusetts
Michigan
Minnesota
Mississippi
Missouri
Montana
Nebraska
Nevada
New Hampshire
New Jersey
New Mexico
New York
```

Figure 4.5: This program returns a state name from the supplied abbreviation (part 3 of 4).

```
North Carolina
North Dakota
Ohio
Oklahoma
Oregon
Pennsylvania
Rhode Island
South Carolina
South Dakota
Tennessee
Texas
Utah
Vermont
Virginia
Washington
West Virginia
Wisconsin
Wyoming
```

Figure 4.5: This program returns a state name from the supplied abbreviation (part 4 of 4).

This very simple ILE RPG program looks up the supplied state abbreviation and returns the corresponding state name. If an invalid state abbreviation is supplied, a return value of '* ERROR' will result. To create the external scalar function associated with this program, use the CREATE FUNCTION statement shown in Figure 4.6.

```
CREATE FUNCTION QGPL.STATENAME(@STAbbr CHAR(2))
RETURNS CHAR (30)
LANGUAGE RPGLE
PARAMETER STYLE DB2SQL
EXTERNAL NAME QGPL.STATENAME
```

Figure 4.6: This statement creates the scalar function STATENAME.

This function allows a user to easily return a state name from a supplied state abbreviation without having to join to a secondary table containing the state names. The SQL SELECT statement shown below could be used to display the state names for all customers in the table CUSTMAST.

```
SELECT QGPL.STATENAME(CMSTTE)
FROM MYLIB.CUSTMAST
```

When this statement is executed, results similar to those shown in Figure 4.7 are
returned.

```
                              Display Data
                                     Data width . . . . . . :        30
     Position to line  . . . . .   _____    Shift to column  . . . . . .   _____
     ....+....1....+....2....+....3
     STATENAME
     South Carolina
     Pennsylvania
     New York
     Washington
     Louisiana
     Iowa
     Pennsylvania
     Wisconsin
     New York
     Texas
     Texas
     Utah
     Illinois
     Pennsylvania
     New Jersey
     Minnesota
                                                                     More...
     F3=Exit     F12=Cancel     F19=Left     F20=Right     F21=Split
```

Figure 4.7: The STATENAME function returns these results.

A similar external function allows us to obtain a full text representation of a given
numeric date. The ILE RPG source for this function is shown in Figure 4.8.

```
*
*  Program: TEXTDATE
*
*  Description: Convert date to full text date
*
*  Compile command: CRTBNDRPG PGM(mylib/TEXTDATE)
*                             SRCFILE(mylib/QRPGLESRC)
*                             SRCRBR(TEXTDATE)
*
DTEXTDATE           PR
*  Input Parameters
*  Input Date Value (MMDDYYYY)
D  inpDate                     8  0
```

Figure 4.8: This function converts a numeric date to a full text date (part 1 of 3).

```
 *  Output Parameters  (Table Output)
 *  Output Text Representation of the Date
D  outDateText                   50     varying
 * Null Indicators For the previous two parameters
D  ni_InDate                     5i 0
D  ni_Output                     5i 0
 * SQL Info
 * SQL State
D  SQLState                      5
 * Function Name
D  FctnName                      517
 * Function Specific Name
D  SpecName                      128
 * Error Message Text
D  SQLMsg                        70     Varying
 * Call Type
D  CallTyp                       10I 0
 *
D SQL_OK          C                      '00000'
D MonthNames      S             10     Dim(12) CTDATA
DTEXTDATE         PI
 *  Input Parameter
D  inDate                        8  0
 *  Output Parameter
D  outTextDate                   50     varying
 * Null Indicators
D  ni_InDate                     5i 0
D  ni_OutTxt                     5i 0
 * SQL Info
D  SQLState                      5
D  FctnName                      517
D  SpecName                      128
D  SQLMsg                        70     Varying
D  CallTyp                       10I 0
 *
D DATE_DS         DS
D    dtMonth              1       2  0
D    dtDay                3       4  0
D    dtYear               5       8  0
D    dtDate               1       8  0
 /free
   SQLState = SQL_OK;
   Test(DE) *USA inDate;
   If %Error;
     outTextDate='*******************************';
   Else;
```

Figure 4.8: This function converts a numeric date to a full text date (part 2 of 3).

93

```
            dtDate = inDate;
            outTextDate = %Trim(MonthNames(dtMonth)) + ' ' +
                          %Char(dtDay) + ',' + %Char(dtYear);
        EndIf;
        *INLR = *ON;
        Return;
      /End-free
** Month Name Compile Time Array
January
February
March
April
May
June
July
August
September
October
November
December
```

Figure 4.8: This function converts a numeric date to a full text date (part 3 of 3).

This program accepts an 8-digit numeric date in the format mmddyyyy. The program uses a simple technique to convert the supplied date into a printable representation. For example, 06012005 is converted to June 1, 2005.

By itself, this ILE RPG program may be useful as an API for use in other applications. When we create an SQL function based on this program, we add greatly to that usefulness. The CREATE FUNCTION statement in Figure 4.9 accomplishes the creation of this function.

```
CREATE FUNCTION MYLIB.TEXTDATE(@INDATE DEC(8,0))
RETURNS VARCHAR (50)
LANGUAGE RPGLE
PARAMETER STYLE DB2SQL
EXTERNAL NAME MYLIB.TEXTDATE
```

Figure 4.9: This statement creates the interface to our TEXTDATE application.

Once the function has been created, we are ready to test it from the interactive SQL command line. The following SELECT statement makes use of the TEXTDATE function.

```
SELECT ORDATE, MYLIB.TEXTDATE(ORDATE) FROM MYLIB.ORDERS
```

In this example, the table ORDERS contains an 8-digit date field, ORDATE, in the format mmddyyyy. When the statement is executed, each row will call the TEXTDATE function to convert the value of the field ORDATE into a text date. Figure 4.10 illustrates what the output from this statement looks like.

```
                              Display Data
                                        Data width . . . . . . :     60
     Position to line  . . . . .   _____     Shift to column  . . . . .   _____
     ....+....1....+....2....+....3....+....4....+....5....+....6
     OLDDATE   TEXTDATE
     11132002  November 13, 2002
     11112002  November 11, 2002
     11112002  November 11, 2002
     11132002  November 13, 2002
     11132002  November 13, 2002
     11122002  November 12, 2002
     11122002  November 12, 2002
     11132002  November 13, 2002
     11122002  November 12, 2002
     04302003  April 30, 2003
     05012003  May 1, 2003
     05012003  May 1, 2003
     04302003  April 30, 2003
     04292003  April 29, 2003
     04302003  April 30, 2003
     05142003  May 14, 2003
                                                              More...

     F3=Exit     F12=Cancel     F19=Left     F20=Right     F21=Split

     b              MW                                        03/032
```

Figure 4.10: This is the output generated by the TEXTDATE function.

As with the prior examples, this function helps to illustrate the ease of using simple applications as SQL functions. Each of the previous examples uses an ILE RPG program as the basis for the scalar function.

The next example I'd like to examine illustrates how to use a CL program as an external scalar function. Figure 4.11 contains the CL source for this example.

```
/*-----------------------------------------------------------------------*/
/*  PROGRAM: GETUSRNAME                                                   */
/*                                                                        */
/*  DESCRIPTION: CL PROGRAM FOR USE AS SQL EXTERNAL SCALAR FUNCTION TO    */
/*               RETRIEVE USER NAME FOR SUPPLIED USER ID                  */
/*                                                                        */
/*  CREATE COMMAND: CRTCLPGM PGM(MYLIB/GETUSRNAME) SRCFILE(MYLIB/QCLSRC)  */
/*                                                                        */
/*-----------------------------------------------------------------------*/
          PGM          PARM(&USERID &USERNAME &UIDIND &UNMIND &SQLSTATE +
                            &FNCNM &SPCNM &DIAGTXT)

          DCL          VAR(&USERID) TYPE(*CHAR) LEN(10) /* Input - +
                            User ID */
          DCL          VAR(&USERNAME) TYPE(*CHAR) LEN(50) /* Output +
                            - User Name */
          DCL          VAR(&UIDIND) TYPE(*DEC) LEN(5 0) /* SQL Null +
                            Indicator */
          DCL          VAR(&UNMIND) TYPE(*DEC) LEN(5 0) /* SQL - +
                            NULL Indicator */
          DCL          VAR(&SQLSTATE) TYPE(*CHAR) LEN(5) /* SQL +
                            State */
          DCL          VAR(&FNCNM) TYPE(*CHAR) LEN(139) /* Function +
                            Name */
          DCL          VAR(&SPCNM) TYPE(*CHAR) LEN(128) /* Specific +
                            Name */
          DCL          VAR(&DIAGTXT) TYPE(*CHAR) LEN(70) /* +
                            Diagnostic Text */

          IF           COND(&USERID *EQ ' ') THEN(CHGVAR +
                            VAR(&USERID) VALUE('*CURRENT')) /* If +
                            User is Blank, Use Current */

          RTVUSRPRF    USRPRF(&USERID) TEXT(&USERNAME)
          MONMSG       MSGID(CPD0078 CPD0079 CPF2204 CPF0001) EXEC(DO)
          CHGVAR       VAR(&USERNAME) VALUE('* USER ID INVALID *')
          CHGVAR       VAR(&DIAGTXT) VALUE('INVALID USER ID')
          ENDDO
          MONMSG       MSGID(CPF2217) EXEC(DO)
          CHGVAR       VAR(&USERNAME) VALUE('* ACCESS DENIED *')
          CHGVAR       VAR(&DIAGTXT) VALUE('ACCESS TO THE SPECIFIED +
                            USER PROFILE HAS BEEN DENIED')
          ENDDO

          ENDPGM
```

Figure 4.11: External scalar functions can also be CL programs.

This application accepts an iSeries user ID and returns the text from the user profile associated with that ID. You'll notice that I have defined a set of additional parameters for null indicators, SQL state, function name, specific name, and diagnostic text. The CREATE FUNCTION statement will require these additional parameters when you specify a parameter type of DB2SQL.

This program uses the RTVUSRPRF command to extract the user text from the user profile supplied on the &USERID variable. The value is passed into the variable &USERNAME, which is then returned to the SQL statement that called the function.

Monitor message (MONMSG) commands are used for error trapping. If the value provided is invalid or if the user executing the SQL statement does not have access to the specified profile, an error message is returned to the caller.

Figure 4.12 contains the CREATE FUNCTION statement that should be used to build the external scalar function using this program.

```
CREATE FUNCTION MYLIB.GETUSERNAME(@USERID CHAR (10))
RETURNS CHAR(50)
LANGUAGE CL
PARAMETER STYLE DB2SQL
EXTERNAL NAME MYLIB.GETUSRNAME
```

Figure 4.12: This statement is used to create the GetUserName function.

After executing this statement, the GetUserName function will be available. This function can be called from an SQL SELECT statement, as shown here:

```
SELECT USERID, MYLIB.GETUSERNAME(USERID)
    FROM MAINTHIST
```

When executed, this statement lists the user ID and associated user profile text from all records in the table MAINTHIST. Figure 4.13 shows a sample of what the output from this statement will look like.

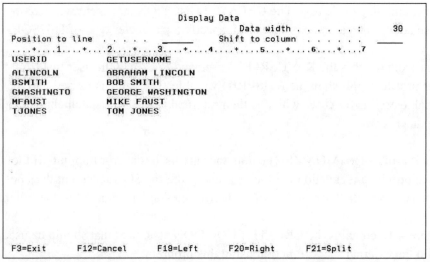

```
                                Display Data
                                        Data width . . . . . . :        30
        Position to line  . . . . .   _____     Shift to column  . . . . . .   _____
        ....+....1....+....2....+....3....+....4....+....5....+....6....+....7
        USERID              GETUSERNAME

        ALINCOLN            ABRAHAM LINCOLN
        BSMITH              BOB SMITH
        GWASHINGTO          GEORGE WASHINGTON
        MFAUST              MIKE FAUST
        TJONES              TOM JONES












        F3=Exit       F12=Cancel      F19=Left      F20=Right      F21=Split
```

Figure 4.13: This is an example of the output generated by the GETUSERNAME function.

As you can see, this function makes it easy to retrieve system-level data into an SQL query.

Each of these examples of external scalar functions returns a single value for each row in which it is called. An external table function allows us to return an entire record set from a single function call.

External Table Functions

As its name suggests, an external table function returns a table. The function name can be used within a FROM clause, as shown:

```
SELECT * FROM MYLIB.MYFUNCTION
```

When the statement is executed, the function is called, and the table data is returned one row at a time. Figure 4.14 shows the syntax of the CREATE FUNCTION statement when used to create an external table function.

```
CREATE FUNCTION function_name (parm1, parm2, etc.)
RETURNS TABLE (field1 type1, field2 type2, etc.)
EXTERAL NAME library.program
LANGUAGE language_name
PARAMETER STYLE parameter definition style
```

Figure 4.14: The example above illustrates the use of CREATE FUNCTION.

You'll notice that the RETURNS modifier has been replaced by RETURNS TABLE. This clause allows us to create the definition for the table data to be returned by the function. Fields within the results table are defined in the same manner used to define the fields using the CREATE TABLE statement—that is, field name followed by field type and length. The CARDINALITY clause can be used to optionally define the number of rows expected to be returned by the table function. This value is supplied as an integer value that follows the CARDINALITY in the clause. The query optimizer uses this function to help improve function performance.

Table functions can be an excellent way to build the equivalent of temporary data files without having to actually store data sets. The ILE RPG source shown in Figure 4.15 will be used to create an external table function.

```
*_____
*
* Program: WEDATES
*
* Description: External Table Function to Return Week Ending Date
*
* Compile Commands: CRTRPGMOD MODULE(xxx/WEDATES)
*                             SRCFILE(xxx/QRPGLESRC)
*                             SRCMBR(WEDATES)
*                   CRTSRVPGM SRVPGM(xxx/WEDATES)
*                             EXPORT(*ALL)
*
*_____
H NOMAIN
DWKENDTS          PR
  *  Input Parameters
D  strDate                    8  0
D  Weeks                      5  0
  *  Output Parameters  (Table Output)
D  weYear                     4  0
```

Figure 4.15: This ILE service program will act as an SQL table function (part 1 of 3).

```
D   weMonth                          2  0
D   weDay                            2  0
D   weDate                           8  0
 *  Null Indicators
D   ni_InDate                       5i  0
D   ni_weeks                        5i  0
D   ni_weyr                         5i  0
D   ni_wemth                        5i  0
D   ni_wedy                         5i  0
D   ni_wedt                         5i  0
 *  SQL Info
D   SQLState                         5
D   FctnName                       517
D   SpecName                       128
D   SQLMsg                          70     Varying
D   CallTyp                        10I  0
 *
D DOWK          S                    2  0
D DATEDS        DS
D   weYrx                   1         4  0
D   weMnx                   5         6  0
D   weDyx                   7         8  0
D   weDtx                   1         8  0
D   weDateA                 1         8
D SQL_OK        C                           '00000'
D SQL_EOF       C                           '02000'

PWKENDTS       B                          Export
DWKENDTS       PI
 *   Input Parameters
D   strDate                          8  0
D   Weeks                            5  0
 *   Output Parameters   (Table Output)
D   weYear                           4  0
D   weMonth                          2  0
D   weDay                            2  0
D   weDate                           8  0
 *  Null Indicators
D   ni_InDate                       5i  0
D   ni_weeks                        5i  0
D   ni_weyr                         5i  0
D   ni_wemth                        5i  0
D   ni_wedy                         5i  0
D   ni_wedt                         5i  0
 *  SQL Info
D   SQLState                         5
D   FctnName                       517
D   SpecName                       128
D   SQLMsg                          70     Varying
D   CallTyp                        10I  0
 *
D strWEDate     S                    D   DATFMT(*ISO) STATIC
```

Figure 4.15: This ILE service program will act as an SQL table function (part 2 of 3).

```
D X                 S               4  0 STATIC
 /free
  SQLState = SQL_OK;
  If X = 0;
   DOWK = %Rem(%Diff(%Date(strDate:*ISO):%Date('1998-08-01'):
         *DAYS): 7);
    If DOWK <= 0;
      DOWK = DOWK + 7;
    EndIF;
    If DOWK = 8;
      DOWK = 0;
    EndIf;
    DOWK = 7 - DOWK;
    strWEDate = %Date(strDate) + %Days(DOWK);
   Else;
    strWEDate = strWEDate + %Days(7);
   EndIf;
   If X <= Weeks;
    weDateA = %CHAR(strWEDate: *ISOO);
    weYear = weYrx;
    weMonth = weMnx;
    weDay = weDyx;
    weDate = weDtx;
    X = X + 1;
   Else;
    *INLR = *ON;
    SQLState = SQL_EOF;
    X = 0;
   EndIf;
   Return;
  /End-free
 PWKENDTS           E
```

Figure 4.15: This ILE service program will act as an SQL table function (part 3 of 3).

The source shown here is used to create an ILE service program. This program accepts two input parameters, which define the start date and the number of weeks to return. The program outputs four return parameters that will act as the columns in our table. In addition to these, there are six other parameters that are used as null indicators for our input and output parameters and five more SQL informational parameters. These parameters provide SQL state information, the function name, the specific name, SQL message text, and a call type value. We are able to use the SQL state parameter to return an end-of-table indicator to the calling application. The program itself takes the input date value in yyyymmdd format and calculates the number of Friday dates supplied on the WEEKS parameter. Each date is returned to the caller as its own record. In addition to this, the function returns the date broken down into year, month, and day fields.

Two steps are required to create the ILE service program above prior to using the CREATE FUNCTION command to build the resulting SQL table function. First, we must build the ILE module, using the Create RPG Module (CRTRPG-MOD) command:

```
CRTRPGMOD MODULE(xxx/WEDATES) SRCFILE(xxx/QRPGLESRC)
    SRCMBR(WEDATES)
```

Once this module has been compiled, you can create the service program using the following command:

```
CRTSRVPGM SRVPGM(MFAUST/WEDATES) EXPORT(*ALL)
```

These two commands prepare the service program, which will be the workhorse of the WeekEndDate function.

Now, we are ready to create the interface to the external SQL table function by using the CREATE FUNCTION command as shown in Figure 4.16.

```
Create Function weekenddates (strDate Decimal(8,0), NumWeeks
Decimal(4,0))
Returns Table(weYear Decimal(4, 0), weMonth Decimal(2, 0),
                weDay Decimal(2, 0),
                weDate Decimal(8, 0))
External Name 'WEDATES(WKENDTS)'
Language RPGLE
Disallow Parallel
No SQL
Parameter Style DB2SQL
Deterministic
```

Figure 4.16: This statement creates our external table function.

You can execute this statement in two ways: by using the interactive SQL function (STRSQL) from the iSeries Navigator SQL script utility that we examined earlier or by saving the source in a source file member and executing the source using the RUNSQLSTM command, which we also examined earlier. Once the table function has been created, you can test the new function from the interactive SQL utility using the following SELECT statement:

```
SELECT * FROM TABLE(MYLIB.WeekEndDates(20050103, 52)) AS
  WeekEndDate
```

This statement returns a list containing week ending (Friday) dates, starting with the Friday after 1/3/2005 and going out 52 weeks. The data shown in Table 4.1 contains a portion of the data returned.

Table 4.1: Sample Data Returned by the WeekEndDates Table Function

WEYEAR	WEMONTH	WEDAY	WEDATE
2005	1	22	20050122
2005	1	29	20050129
2005	2	5	20050205
2005	2	12	20050212
2005	2	19	20050219
2005	2	26	20050226
2005	3	5	20050305
2005	3	12	20050312
2005	3	19	20050319
2005	3	26	20050326
2005	4	2	20050402

This sample function shows the usefulness of user-defined table functions. In this case, we can generate dates out almost an unlimited number of weeks without having to store this data anywhere. Since these values are easily calculated and can be easily recalculated, there is no reason to statically store this data. The user-defined table function allows us access to these types of calculated values in the same way we can access any other SQL table.

SQL Scalar Functions

We've already explored how to create a user-defined function using an application written in a non-SQL language. Now let's take a look at the same process using a function written in SQL. When the resulting function is an SQL function, the syntax used for the CREATE FUNCTION statement is similar to what it was when we created our external user-defined function earlier. Figure 4.17 below shows the syntax used to create an SQL function.

```
CREATE FUNCTION function_name (parm1, parm2, etc.)
RETURNS return_type
LANGUAGE SQL
CONTAINS SQL
BEGIN
  ... function body
RETURN return_value
END
```

Figure 4.17: This syntax is used to create a user-defined SQL scalar function.

The key difference here is that the CREATE FUNCTION statement and its modifiers are followed by the BEGIN, RETURN, and END statements. When creating a function, the BEGIN and END statements allow us to use a group of SQL statements within our procedure. It's also possible, however, to create a function that uses a single SQL statement to evaluate the function's result. The function shown in Figure 4.18 is an example of this type of SQL scalar function.

```
CREATE FUNCTION CustName(CUSN CHAR(8))
RETURNS CHAR(35)
LANGUAGE SQL
READS SQL DATA
RETURN (SELECT CUSNAM FROM CUSTMAST WHERE CNCUSN = CUSN)
```

Figure 4.18: This scalar SQL function returns a value from a single SELECT.

This function uses the single supplied parameter to retrieve a single field from a specific record in the defined file. This type of function can save us from having to perform a join operation to grab a single field from a table. In this example, our function selects a customer name value for the supplied customer number.

This is probably the simplest form of SQL scalar function. Functions of a more complex nature can be created using the SQL procedural language we examined in chapter 3. A sample of this type of function is shown in Figure 4.19.

```
CREATE FUNCTION QGPL.GETMILES(@ORIGZIP VARCHAR(5),@DESTZIP
    VARCHAR(5), @UNIT VARCHAR(1))
RETURNS DECIMAL(13,0)
LANGUAGE SQL
BEGIN
        DECLARE @PI FLOAT;
        DECLARE @X FLOAT;
        DECLARE @DISTANCE FLOAT;
        DECLARE @LAT1 FLOAT;
        DECLARE @LAT2 FLOAT;
        DECLARE @LONG1 FLOAT;
        DECLARE @LONG2 FLOAT;

        SELECT LAT, "LONG" INTO @LAT1, @LONG1
        FROM QGPL.ZIPCODES WHERE ZIPCD = @ORIGZIP;
        SELECT LAT, "LONG" INTO @LAT2, @LONG2
        FROM QGPL.ZIPCODES WHERE ZIPCD = @DESTZIP;

        SET @PI=3.1415927;
        SET @X = (SIN((@LAT1 * @PI/180)) * SIN((@LAT2* @PI/180))
                + COS((@LAT1* @PI/180)) * COS((@LAT2* @PI/180))
                * COS(ABS((((@LONG2* @PI/180))-((@LONG1*@PI/180))))
        SET @X = ATAN((SQRT(1-(@X*@X)))/@X);
        SET @DISTANCE = (1.852 * 60.0 * ((@X/@PI)*180));
        IF (UPPER(@UNIT)='M') THEN
                SET @DISTANCE = (@DISTANCE * .621371192);
        ELSE
                IF (UPPER(@UNIT)='N') THEN
                        SET @DISTANCE = (@DISTANCE * 0.539956803);
                END IF;
        END IF;
        RETURN @DISTANCE;
END
```

Figure 4.19: SQL scalar functions can perform complex calculations.

This example creates an SQL function that will calculate distance between two postal ZIP codes. You'll note that the field name LONG in this example is enclosed in quotes. This must be done because LONG is a reserved word in the SQL language. We're able to get around this problem by enclosing the value in quotes. The function itself requires a ZIP code database that is used to cross-reference a given ZIP code to its longitude and latitude values. A version of this database has been included with the companion code to this book; however, the data contained in this database is not guaranteed to be up-to-date and complete. The GetMiles function accepts the following three input parameters:

- Five-character origin ZIP code

- Five-character destination ZIP code

- Unit-of-measure value

The unit of measure is included to identify whether the value returned should represent kilometers (which is the default value), miles (represented by 'M'), or nautical miles (represented by 'N'). The function retrieves the longitude and latitude values for the supplied ZIP codes from the table QGPL.ZIPCODES. The function then uses spherical geometry to calculate the distance between those two points. It's important to realize that the value returned is a straight-line, point-to-point distance, not a driving distance. In any case, the function is an excellent example of using SQL procedural language to build a user-defined function that performs complex calculations. Figure 4.20 shows how you would use this function within an SQL SELECT statement.

```
SELECT SHPZIP, QGPL.GETMILES(32771, SHPZIP, 'M') AS DIST,
QGPL.GETMILES(32771, DZIP, 'M') * RTPRMI AS FRTCST
FROM ORDERS INNER JOIN CARRIERS ON ORDERS.CARR = CARRIERS.CARR
```

Figure 4.20: Use the GetMiles function within an SQL SELECT statement.

This statement uses the GetMiles function to calculate the distance between the ZIP code 32771 and the ZIP code identified in the field SHPZIP. The statement then takes this distance value and multiplies it by a value that represents a rate-per-mile (RTPRMI) value to calculate a freight cost for the ORDERS record. This function can also be used within an ORDER BY clause to list locations closest to a specified location. The statement in Figure 4.21 illustrates this.

```
SELECT STRZIP, QGPL.GETMILES(32771, STRZIP, 'M') AS DIST
FROM STORES
WHERE QGPL.GETMILES(32771, STRZIP, 'M') < 50
ORDER BY QGPL.GETMILES(32771, STRZIP, 'M')
```

Figure 4.21: Use the GetMiles function as part of an ORDER BY clause.

Assuming that the table STORES contains addresses of stores and that the field STRZIP contains the ZIP codes for each of these stores, the statement above will return a listing of stores within 50 miles of the ZIP code 32771 in order from closest to farthest. Below is a sample of the output generated by this function:

Zip Code	DIST
32746	4
32713	6
32725	7
32708	8
32750	8
32707	10

Let's examine one more SQL scalar function. The source for this function is shown in Figure 4.22.

```
CREATE FUNCTION QGPL.PhnLtrToNum(STRINGIN VARCHAR(50))
RETURNS VARCHAR(50)
LANGUAGE SQL
BEGIN
     DECLARE X INT;
     DECLARE RET VARCHAR(50);
     DECLARE CHR VARCHAR(1);
     DECLARE CH2 VARCHAR(1);
     SET X=1;
     WHILE X <= LENGTH(TRIM(STRINGIN)) DO
     SET CHR='';
     SET CH2=UPPER(SUBSTR(STRINGIN,X,1));
     CASE
        WHEN POSSTR('ABC', CH2)>0 THEN
            SET CHR='2';
```

Figure 4.22: This is another example of an SQL scalar function (part 1 of 2).

```
                WHEN POSSTR('DEF', CH2)>0 THEN
                    SET CHR='3';
                WHEN POSSTR('GHI', CH2)>0 THEN

                    SET CHR='4';
                WHEN POSSTR('JKL', CH2)>0 THEN
                    SET CHR='5';
                WHEN POSSTR('MNO', CH2)>0 THEN
                    SET CHR='6';
                WHEN POSSTR('PQRS', CH2)>0 THEN
                    SET CHR='7';
                WHEN POSSTR('TUV', CH2)>0 THEN
                    SET CHR='8';
                WHEN POSSTR('WXYZ', CH2)>0 THEN
                    SET CHR='9';
                WHEN POSSTR('0123456789', CH2)>0   THEN
                    SET CHR=SUBSTR(STRINGIN,X,1);
                ELSE
                    SET CHR='';
                END CASE;
            IF CHR <> '' THEN
            IF X = 1 THEN
            SET RET=CHR;
            ELSE SET RET=TRIM(RET)||TRIM(CHR);
            END IF;
            END IF;
            SET X=X+1;
            END WHILE;
            RETURN TRIM(RET);
    END
```

Figure 4.22: This is another example of an SQL scalar function (part 2 of 2).

The function PhnLtrToNum converts the string provided on the function's only parameter into a string of corresponding numeric values. Each alpha character within the string is converted to the number on which the letter appears on a standard telephone keypad. This function can be useful from within interactive voice response (IVR) applications that require a user to enter alphanumeric search criteria through a telephone. The function can take an alphanumeric string—a person's last name, for example—and convert the string into a string containing the corresponding numeric value. Figure 4.23 shows an example of this conversion.

Figure 4.23: This illustration shows how phone letter conversion works.

As this illustrates, the letters for the name FAUST would be converted to 32878. As a result, a user would be able to search a data set that used this function by the numeric value 32878.

The SQL statement in Figure 4.24 returns a list of all records in the table CUSTOMERS where the field LASTNAME converts to the value 76484. As a result, any customers with the last name SMITH will be listed.

```
SELECT *
FROM CUSTOMERS
WHERE QGPL.PhnLtrToNum(LASTNAME) = '76484'
```

Figure 4.24 This statement utilizes the PhnLtrToNum SQL scalar function.

When this statement is executed, a list of customers matching the numeric pattern specified is returned. In this case, the numeric value is a match for the name SMITH. Below is a sample of the output that is generated.

Last Name	First Name	Middle Name
SMITH	CAROLANN	
SMITH	JOHN	A
SMITH	JOHN	S
SMITH	JAMES	N
SMITH	MIKE	ANDREW
SMITH	NANCY	L
SMITH	PEGGY	A
SMITH	EOAN	A

The final example of an SQL scalar function that I'd like to explore with you will allow you to express a number in written dollar form. Using this function, we are able to convert this number

```
1,158,432.75
```

to this text

```
One million, one hundred fifty eight thousand four hundred
thirty two dollars and 75 cents
```

This function accepts a value from -999999999 to 999999999. The source for this SQL function is shown in Figure 4.25

```
CREATE FUNCTION QGPL.TEXTDOLLARS (@INNUMBER DECIMAL(11, 2))
RETURNS VARCHAR(128)
LANGUAGE SQL
SPECIFIC QGPL.TEXTDOLLARS
NOT DETERMINISTIC
READS SQL DATA
CALLED ON NULL INPUT
DISALLOW PARALLEL
BEGIN
       DECLARE CENTS DECIMAL(2 ,2);
       DECLARE CHARINT CHAR(9);
       DECLARE DOLLARTEXT VARCHAR(128);
       DECLARE TEMP CHAR( 3 ) ;
       DECLARE Y INTEGER;

       SET Y = 1;
       SET CENTS = @INNUMBER - INT(@INNUMBER);
       SET CHARINT = RIGHT(TRIM('000000000' || CHAR(INT(@INNUMBER))) , 9 ;
       SET DOLLARTEXT = '';
       WHILE Y < 9 DO
       SET TEMP = SUBSTR(CHARINT, Y, 3);
       CASE SUBSTR(TEMP,1 ,1)
       WHEN '1' THEN
              SET DOLLARTEXT = TRIM(DOLLARTEXT) || ' ONE HUNDRED' ;
       WHEN '2' THEN
              SET DOLLARTEXT = TRIM(DOLLARTEXT) || ' TWO HUNDRED' ;
       WHEN '3' THEN
              SET DOLLARTEXT = TRIM(DOLLARTEXT) || ' THREE HUNDRED' ;
       WHEN '4' THEN
              SET DOLLARTEXT = TRIM(DOLLARTEXT) || ' FOUR HUNDRED' ;
       WHEN '5' THEN
              SET DOLLARTEXT = TRIM(DOLLARTEXT) || ' FIVE HUNDRED' ;
       WHEN '6' THEN
              SET DOLLARTEXT = TRIM(DOLLARTEXT) || ' SIX HUNDRED' ;
       WHEN '7' THEN
              SET DOLLARTEXT = TRIM(DOLLARTEXT)|| ' SEVEN HUNDRED' ;
       WHEN '8' THEN
              SET DOLLARTEXT = TRIM(DOLLARTEXT)|| ' EIGHT HUNDRED' ;
       WHEN '9' THEN
              SET DOLLARTEXT = TRIM(DOLLARTEXT)|| ' NINE HUNDRED' ;
       ELSE
              SET DOLLARTEXT = TRIM(DOLLARTEXT);
       END CASE ;
```

Figure 4.25: This function converts a number to a text dollar amount (part 1 of 3).

110

```
IF SUBSTR ( TEMP , 2 , 1 ) = '1' THEN
CASE SUBSTR ( TEMP , 2 , 2 )

WHEN '10' THEN
        SET DOLLARTEXT = TRIM(DOLLARTEXT)|| ' TEN ' ;
WHEN '11' THEN
        SET DOLLARTEXT = TRIM(DOLLARTEXT)|| ' ELEVEN ' ;
WHEN '12' THEN
        SET DOLLARTEXT = TRIM(DOLLARTEXT)|| ' TWELVE ' ;
WHEN '13' THEN
        SET DOLLARTEXT = TRIM(DOLLARTEXT)|| ' THIRTEEN ' ;
WHEN '14' THEN
        SET DOLLARTEXT = TRIM(DOLLARTEXT)|| ' FOURTEEN ' ;
WHEN '15' THEN
        SET DOLLARTEXT = TRIM(DOLLARTEXT)|| ' FIFTEEN ' ;
WHEN '16' THEN
        SET DOLLARTEXT = TRIM(DOLLARTEXT)|| ' SIXTEEN ' ;
WHEN '17' THEN
        SET DOLLARTEXT = TRIM(DOLLARTEXT)|| ' SEVENTEEN ' ;
WHEN '18' THEN
        SET DOLLARTEXT = TRIM(DOLLARTEXT)|| ' EIGHTTEEN ' ;
WHEN '19' THEN
        SET DOLLARTEXT = TRIM(DOLLARTEXT)|| ' NINETEEN ' ;
ELSE
SET DOLLARTEXT = TRIM(DOLLARTEXT);
END CASE ;
ELSE
CASE SUBSTR ( TEMP , 2 , 1 )
WHEN '2' THEN
        SET DOLLARTEXT = TRIM(DOLLARTEXT)|| ' TWENTY ' ;
WHEN '3' THEN
        SET DOLLARTEXT = TRIM(DOLLARTEXT)|| ' THIRTY ' ;
WHEN '4' THEN
        SET DOLLARTEXT = TRIM(DOLLARTEXT)|| ' FORTY ' ;
WHEN '5' THEN
        SET DOLLARTEXT = TRIM(DOLLARTEXT)|| ' FIFTY ' ;
WHEN '6' THEN
        SET DOLLARTEXT = TRIM(DOLLARTEXT)|| ' SIXTY ' ;
WHEN '7' THEN
        SET DOLLARTEXT = TRIM(DOLLARTEXT)|| ' SEVENTY ' ;
WHEN '8' THEN
        SET DOLLARTEXT = TRIM(DOLLARTEXT)|| ' EIGHTY ' ;
WHEN '9' THEN
        SET DOLLARTEXT = TRIM(DOLLARTEXT)|| ' NINETY ' ;
ELSE
        SET DOLLARTEXT = TRIM(DOLLARTEXT);
END CASE ;
CASE SUBSTR ( TEMP , 3 , 1 )
```

Figure 4.25: This function converts a number to a text dollar amount (part 2 of 3).

```
            WHEN '1' THEN

                    SET DOLLARTEXT = TRIM(DOLLARTEXT)|| ' ONE ' ;
            WHEN '2' THEN
                    SET DOLLARTEXT = TRIM(DOLLARTEXT)|| ' TWO ' ;
            WHEN '3' THEN
                    SET DOLLARTEXT = TRIM(DOLLARTEXT)|| ' THREE ' ;
            WHEN '4' THEN
                    SET DOLLARTEXT = TRIM(DOLLARTEXT)|| ' FOUR ' ;
            WHEN '5' THEN
                    SET DOLLARTEXT = TRIM(DOLLARTEXT)|| ' FIVE ' ;
            WHEN '6' THEN
                    SET DOLLARTEXT = TRIM(DOLLARTEXT)|| ' SIX ' ;
            WHEN '7' THEN
                    SET DOLLARTEXT = TRIM(DOLLARTEXT)|| ' SEVEN ' ;
            WHEN '8' THEN
                    SET DOLLARTEXT = TRIM(DOLLARTEXT)|| ' EIGHT ' ;
            WHEN '9' THEN
                    SET DOLLARTEXT = TRIM(DOLLARTEXT)|| ' NINE ' ;
            ELSE
                    SET DOLLARTEXT = TRIM(DOLLARTEXT);
            END CASE ;
            END IF ;
            CASE Y
            WHEN 1 THEN
            IF TEMP <> '000' AND TEMP <> '' THEN
                    SET DOLLARTEXT = TRIM(DOLLARTEXT)|| ' MILLION ' ;
            END IF ;
            WHEN 4 THEN
            IF TEMP <> '000' AND TEMP <> '' THEN
                    SET DOLLARTEXT = TRIM(DOLLARTEXT)|| ' THOUSAND ' ;
            END IF ;
            ELSE
                    SET DOLLARTEXT = TRIM(DOLLARTEXT);
            END CASE ;
                    SET Y = Y + 3 ;
            END WHILE ;
            IF @INNUMBER<1 THEN
                    SET DOLLARTEXT = TRIM(DOLLARTEXT) || ' ZERO ';
            END IF;
            IF @INNUMBER>=1 AND @INNUMBER<2 THEN
                    SET DOLLARTEXT = TRIM(DOLLARTEXT)|| ' DOLLAR AND ';
            ELSE
                    SET DOLLARTEXT = TRIM(DOLLARTEXT)|| ' DOLLARS AND ';
            END IF;
            SET DOLLARTEXT=TRIM(DOLLARTEXT)||' '||TRIM(DIGITS(CENTS))||' CENTS ';
            RETURN DOLLARTEXT;
    END;
```

Figure 4.25: This function converts a number to a text dollar amount (part 3 of 3).

This function performs a task that you probably have the code to accomplish somewhere on your iSeries now. However, building this into an SQL function gives you the simplicity of being able to calculate this value on the fly. The following statement uses this function within an SQL SELECT.

```
SELECT QGPL.TEXTDOLLARS(CHQAMT)
FROM MYLIB.CHECKFILE
WHERE CHQAMT <> 0
```

This statement selects all records from the table CHECKFILE where the check amount field is not 0 and displays the text dollar representation of the check amount. When executed, this statement will return a list similar to that shown in Figure 4.26.

```
                                        Display Data
                                                             Data width . . . . . . :    128
Position to line  . . . . .    _____                          Shift to column  . . . . . .   ____
....+....1....+....2....+....3....+....4....+....5....+....6....+....7....+....8....+....9....+...10....+...11....+...12....+...
TEXTDOLLARS
THREE HUNDRED THOUSAND DOLLARS AND 00 CENTS
TWO HUNDRED THOUSAND DOLLARS AND 00 CENTS
FIFTY THOUSAND DOLLARS AND 00 CENTS
NINETY EIGHT THOUSAND TWO HUNDRED FOURTEEN DOLLARS AND 58 CENTS
NINETY NINE THOUSAND NINE HUNDRED THIRTY THREE DOLLARS AND 33 CENTS
SIX HUNDRED TWENTY EIGHT DOLLARS AND 89 CENTS
NINETEEN THOUSAND NINETY EIGHT DOLLARS AND 00 CENTS
ELEVEN THOUSAND FOUR HUNDRED THIRTY DOLLARS AND 21 CENTS
FOURTEEN THOUSAND THREE HUNDRED EIGHTY FOUR DOLLARS AND 13 CENTS
ELEVEN THOUSAND ONE HUNDRED NINETY NINE DOLLARS AND 22 CENTS
TEN THOUSAND DOLLARS AND 00 CENTS
NINE THOUSAND EIGHT HUNDRED FOURTY ONE DOLLARS AND 11 CENTS
NINETEEN THOUSAND SIX HUNDRED EIGHTY SIX DOLLARS AND 60 CENTS
TEN THOUSAND DOLLARS AND 00 CENTS
SIXTY THOUSAND DOLLARS AND 00 CENTS
FIFTEEN THOUSAND DOLLARS AND 00 CENTS
TWENTY NINE THOUSAND DOLLARS AND 00 CENTS
FIVE THOUSAND DOLLARS AND 00 CENTS
TEN THOUSAND DOLLARS AND 00 CENTS
                                                                                    More...
F3=Exit      F12=Cancel      F19=Left      F20=Right      F21=Split      F22=Width 80
```

Figure 4.26: The TEXTDOLLARS function generates this output.

Each of these examples helps to illustrate the flexibility of using SQL procedural language to create user-defined scalar functions. This flexibility also comes into play when creating SQL user-defined table functions.

SQL Table Functions

As with external functions, we can create user-defined functions within SQL that return a table as a result set. Figure 4.27 shows the general syntax used to create an SQL table function.

```
CREATE FUNCTION function_name (parm1, parm2, etc.)
RETURNS TABLE(field1type, field2type, etc.)
LANGUAGE SQL
READS SQL
RETURN SELECT field1, field2, etc. FROM MYLIB.MYTABLE
```

Figure 4.27 This is the syntax used to create an SQL table function.

While this syntax is similar to that used to create an SQL scalar function, the key differences are found in the RETURNS TABLE clause and the fact that the RETURNS statement contains multiple return parameters. This type of function can be used to simplify data retrieval in much the same way you would use a view or logical file but with the added flexibility through the use of parameters to dynamically filter the data returned. Figure 4.28 contains the source to a simple SQL table function.

```
CREATE FUNCTION MYLIB.GETFIELDS(@TABLENAME VARCHAR(10),
                @LIBNAME VARCHAR(10))
RETURNS TABLE (FILE VARCHAR(10), FILE_TYPE CHAR(1),
FIELD VARCHAR(10), TYPE VARCHAR(10)
      ,DESCRIPTION VARCHAR(50), FIELD_LENGTH INTEGER)
LANGUAGE SQL
DISALLOW PARALLEL
RETURN SELECT A.TABLE_NAME,B.TABLE_TYPE,A.COLUMN_NAME,A.DATA_TYPE,
        A.COLUMN_TEXT, A.LENGTH
FROM QSYS2.SYSCOLUMNS A INNER JOIN QSYS2.SYSTABLES B ON
        A.TABLE_NAME = B.TABLE_NAME AND
          A.TABLE_SCHEMA=B.TABLE_SCHEMA
   WHERE A.TABLE_NAME = @TABLENAME and A.TABLE_SCHEMA = @LIBNAME
```

Figure 4.28 This is the syntax used to create an SQL table function.

This function accepts a TABLENAME parameter along with a LIBNAME parameter. These two parameters retrieve the table and column data for the specified file. The function returns column and table data for that file as a table function. To initiate this function, use the following SQL SELECT statement:

```
SELECT * FROM TABLE(MYLIB.GETFIELDS('SYSVIEWS','QSYS2')) AS A
```

When called, this function returns a list of the fields in the view SYSVIEWS. A sample of the data returned is shown in Figure 4.29.

```
                              Display Data
                                                   Data width . . . . . . :     113
Position to line . . . . .  _____                  Shift to column . . . . .
....+....1....+....2....+....3....+....4....+....5....+....6....+....7....+....8....+....9....+....10....+...11...
FILE        FILE_TYPE  FIELD       TYPE     DESCR00001                  FIELD00001
SYSVIEWS        V      TABLE_NAME  VARCHAR  Long file name                     128
SYSVIEWS        V      VIEW_OWNER  VARCHAR  -                                  128
SYSVIEWS        V      SEQNO       INTEGER  -                                    4
SYSVIEWS        V      CHECK_OPTI  CHAR     -                                    1
SYSVIEWS        V      VIEW_DEFIN  VARCHAR  SQL VIEW definition              10,000
SYSVIEWS        V      IS_UPDATAB  CHAR     Y-Yes, N-No                          1
SYSVIEWS        V      TABLE_SCHE  VARCHAR  Library name                       128
SYSVIEWS        V      SYSTEM_VIE  CHAR     File name                           10
SYSVIEWS        V      SYSTEM_VIE  CHAR     Library name                        10
SYSVIEWS        V      IS_INSERTA  VARCHAR  -                                    3
SYSVIEWS        V      IASP_NUMBE  SMALLINT Primary ASP                          2
********  End of data  ********

                                                                          Bottom
F3=Exit    F12=Cancel    F19=Left    F20=Right    F21=Split    F22=Width 80
```

Figure 4.29: The SQL table function GetFields outputs this data.

You'll notice that we've combined field data from two distinct tables into our table function. We have also only returned records where the TABLE_NAME and TABLE_SCHEMA values match the parameters passed into the function. This process can greatly simplify the use of complex SELECT statements from other applications. Rather than having to constantly use complex joins to re-create SELECT statements containing several tables, we can just create an SQL table function once and call the function from the end application. In chapter 5, we'll explore taking this function and others like it and using them embedded within RPG programs, Active Server Page (ASP) applications, and even Java programs.

Sourced Functions

Sourced SQL functions allow us to redefine an existing function, either built-in or user-defined, using a different name and/or different parameter type. The existing function can be either a scalar or a columnar function; however, table functions cannot be sourced functions. This type of function is generally used when you need an existing function to conform to other needs. Those needs may be related to data type issues, where you require a parameter or return value to be a different data type than that required or supplied by the existing function. The need can also be more aesthetic, where you simply want to give an existing function a more descriptive name, for example. Function naming can also come into play when converting code from a different SQL dialect, such as Microsoft SQL, for use with the iSeries. In this case, you can create sourced versions of the DB2 SQL functions that match their SQL Server counterparts.

115

As you would imagine, the CREATE FUNCTION statement for a sourced function is much simpler than the statements we've examined to create other functions. Figure 4.30 shows the syntax used to create a sourced function.

```
CREATE FUNCTION functionname (Parm1_type, Parm2_type)
        RETURNS return_parm_type
        SPECIFIC sourced_function_specific_name
        SOURCE existing_function_name (Parm_1_type, Parm_2_type)
                SPECIFIC existing_function_specific_name
```

Figure 4.30: This is the required syntax to create a sourced SQL function.

There is one key difference between this statement and the other CREATE FUNCTION statements we've examined so far. The SOURCE modifier is used to point to the original function to be used as the model for our new function. In this example, you'll notice that parameter definitions can be supplied for the new sourced function as well as for the existing function. This is done to allow for the differences in data type between the sourced function and the original function. The example shown in Figure 4.31 creates a sourced function based on the INT function, which returns a string value.

```
CREATE FUNCTION STRINGINT(DOUBLE)
        RETURNS VARCHAR
        SOURCE INT(DOUBLE)
```

Figure 4.31: This sourced SQL function is based on the INT built-in function.

Once this statement is executed, we can test our new sourced SQL function by entering the interactive SQL command interface and typing the following statement.

```
SELECT STRINGINT(DOUBLE(12345.66))
        FROM QSYS2/SYSFUNCS
```

Note that I am using the DOUBLE function to ensure that the value passed to our sourced function matches that required by the function definition. Again, here I am using QSYS/SYSFUNCS as a dummy data source. When the statement is executed, the data shown in Figure 4.32 is returned.

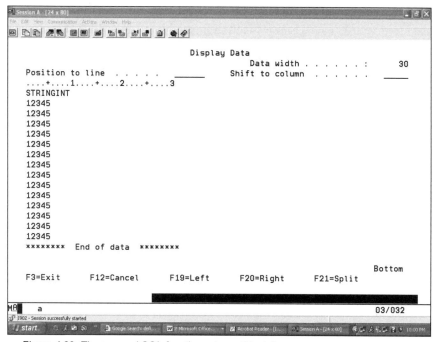

Figure 4.32: The sourced SQL function returns this data.

Note that the decimal places are dropped from the value before it's converted to a type CHAR(30).

As I mentioned earlier, it's also possible to create a sourced function based on a user-defined function. The statement shown in Figure 4.33 creates a sourced function based on the EDITCODE function we created earlier.

```
CREATE FUNCTION MYNEWLIB.EDITCODE(NUMERIC (15,5) VARCHAR(1))
       RETURNS VARCHAR (30)
       SOURCE MYLIB.EDITCODE(NUMERIC (15,5) VARCHAR(1))
```

Figure 4.33: Create a source function based on a user-defined function.

This example creates a redefined version of our first user-defined function example. The sourced version of this function now resides in a different library and returns a data type of VARCHAR rather than the CHAR type returned by the original function. This function helps to illustrate how a sourced function can be used to give users access to a function housed in a library that they would not otherwise have access to. If, for example, a user needs access to the EDITCODE function but doesn't have access to the library MYLIB, the example above can be used to create a sourced version of the function that resides in a library to which the user does have access.

Beyond UDFs

In this chapter, we've explored creating several different types of user-defined functions. We've examined simple and complex functions created in host languages and SQL, as well as functions that return a single value or an entire data set. In chapter 5, we'll cover how to use procedures and functions we've already explored.

5

Using Functions and Procedures

Now that we've explored what functions and procedures can do and how to create them, we'll explore the wide range of ways to make use of the procedures and function samples from this book.

Interactive SQL

In the previous chapters, we made use of the STRSQL interactive SQL command. This powerful utility can be a great tool for performing ad hoc queries and file updates. Stored procedures and user-defined functions can be utilized from within the interactive SQL command line. This ability allows you to extend the usefulness of this utility by extending the existing functionality based on your needs.

In earlier chapters, we ran most of the examples we explored simply to display information to the green-screen, but there are other options for what to do with the output from a function or stored procedure. For example, we can use the Crosstab stored procedure we created in chapter 3 to create an output file. To do this from within the interactive SQL console, we need to change the output option by navigating to the options screen, using the F13 key to change the output to option 3 (output to file), and specifying the file name. This screen is shown in Figure 5.1. If you've ever used Query/400, this screen should look somewhat familiar to you.

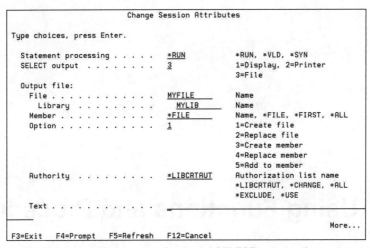

```
                       Change Session Attributes

Type choices, press Enter.

        Statement processing . . . . .   *RUN          *RUN, *VLD, *SYN
        SELECT output . . . . . . . .    3             1=Display, 2=Printer
                                                       3=File
        Output file:
          File . . . . . . . . . . . .   MYFILE        Name
             Library . . . . . . . . .   MYLIB         Name
          Member . . . . . . . . . . .   *FILE         Name, *FILE, *FIRST, *ALL
          Option . . . . . . . . . . .   1             1=Create file
                                                       2=Replace file
                                                       3=Create member
                                                       4=Replace member
                                                       5=Add to member
        Authority . . . . . . . . . .    *LIBCRTAUT    Authorization list name
                                                       *LIBCRTAUT, *CHANGE, *ALL
                                                       *EXCLUDE, *USE

        Text . . . . . . . . . . . .     _

                                                                      More...
 F3=Exit    F4=Prompt    F5=Refresh    F12=Cancel
```

Figure 5.1: Use this screen to change the SELECT output option.

Once we've changed this option, any output generated by the statement entered on the command line will be sent to the file specified. If, for example, we call the Crosstab stored procedure using this option, the output is sent to the file we specified earlier. This allows us to take the data created from our Crosstab query and save it for later.

As you can see, this screen also allows the option of sending the output to a printer, which means that we can use this utility to generate output the same way we would use Query/400. While this utility is powerful, the fact that it can only be used interactively limits its usefulness. There are other options, however.

Query Manager

Query Manager on the iSeries is a more functional version of Query/400. It gives you the ability to create complex reports, using SQL to define the data to appear in the report. This means that, within a Query Manager report, you can use SQL functions, including table functions like the WeekEndDates function we explored in chapter 4. To enter Query Manager, type the command STRQM from the command line. The Query Manager menu is shown in Figure 5.2.

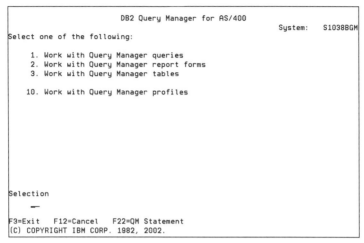

Figure 5.2: This menu is used to access Query Manager.

The two basic parts of a report in Query Manager are the Query Manager query, which describes your data, and the Query Manager report form, which formats the report. The Query Manager query is simply an SQL statement that defines the data that appears on the report and the file (or files) containing this data. The Query Manager report form defines page formatting, such as page headings, column headings, column formatting, subtotals, groupings, and level-break text. Think of the Query Manager query as the right side of the brain and the Query Manager report form as the left side.

Within a Query Manager query, we can incorporate any SQL function, including user-defined scalar functions and table functions. When calling a user-defined function from within Query Manager, it's important to remember that if the *SYS naming convention is used, the function must be accessible from your current library list. When using the SQL naming standard, which is defined as *SAA in Query Manager, the fully qualified function name must be specified as Library Function. To define the naming standard used in Query Manager, take option 10 (Work with Query Manager profiles) from the Query Manager main menu. UDFs can be called from within prompted query creation mode through the Define Expressions panel to define a report column containing a UDF or through the Select Records panel to filter data based on a UDF. For our example, however, we need to use SQL query creation mode. The query creation mode is displayed on the top of the Work with Query Manager Queries display. If the mode shows as PROMPT, use the F19 key to switch to SQL mode. To create a new Query Manager query, take option 1 from the menu shown in Figure 5.2. Now use option 1 to create a new query. The screen displayed, which is shown in Figure 5.3, looks very similar to the SEU screen.

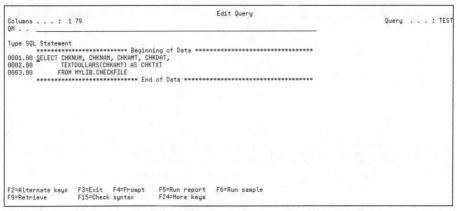

Figure 5.3: This screen is used to edit the SQL for a Query Manager query.

You'll notice that the SQL statements shown on this screen use the TextDollars function we created in chapter 4. When this Query Manager query is combined with a Query Manager report form, the printed output can be generated for a check. Figure 5.4 gives a sample of the output that this statement would generate.

```
                                              Display Report
Query . . . . .:     TEST                 Width . . .:      246
Form . . . . .:      *SYSDFT              Column  . .:        1
Control . . . .
Line       ....+....1....+....2....+....3....+....4....+....5....+....6....+....7....+....8....+....9....+....0....+....1....+....2...
           CHKNUM    CHKNAM                    CHKAMT   CHKDAT     CHKTXT
           --------- ---------------------  ----------- ---------- ----------------------------------------------------------------
  000018   0000066   SMITH, ABIGAIL M        10,144.26  05/01/2005  TEN THOUSAND ONE HUNDRED FOURTY FOUR DOLLARS AND 26 CENTS
  000019   0000067   SMITH, ALEXANDER R      10,144.26  05/01/2005  TEN THOUSAND ONE HUNDRED FOURTY FOUR DOLLARS AND 26 CENTS
  000020   0000068   JONES, AMALEE           10,144.26  05/01/2005  TEN THOUSAND ONE HUNDRED FOURTY FOUR DOLLARS AND 26 CENTS
  000021   0000069   JONES, ANGELA           10,144.26  05/01/2005  TEN THOUSAND ONE HUNDRED FOURTY FOUR DOLLARS AND 26 CENTS
  000022   0000070   JONES, BEVERLY S        10,144.26  05/01/2005  TEN THOUSAND ONE HUNDRED FOURTY FOUR DOLLARS AND 26 CENTS
  000023   0000075   JONES, BRYAN D          10,144.26  05/01/2005  TEN THOUSAND ONE HUNDRED FOURTY FOUR DOLLARS AND 26 CENTS
  000024   0000083   JONES, ALICE            10,144.26  05/01/2005  TEN THOUSAND ONE HUNDRED FOURTY FOUR DOLLARS AND 26 CENTS
  000025   0000135   JONES, BRYAN D              20.01  05/01/2005  TWENTY DOLLARS AND 01 CENTS
  000026   0000136   SMITH, ABIGAIL M           100.23  05/01/2005  ONE HUNDRED DOLLARS AND 23 CENTS
  000027   0000140   SMITH, ALVIN R             360.84  05/01/2005  THREE HUNDRED SIXTY DOLLARS AND 84 CENTS
  000028   0000141   JONES, BENJAMIN F          120.28  05/01/2005  ONE HUNDRED TWENTY DOLLARS AND 28 CENTS
  000029   0000143   SMITH, ARTHUR L          7,517.57  05/01/2005  SEVEN THOUSAND FIVE HUNDRED SEVENTEEN DOLLARS AND 57 CENTS
  000030   0000146   SMITH, ABIGAIL M           451.05  05/01/2005  FOUR HUNDRED FIFTY ONE DOLLARS AND 05 CENTS
  000031   0000147   SMITH,ANNETTE RENEE      6,014.05  05/01/2005  SIX THOUSAND FOURTEEN DOLLARS AND 05 CENTS
  000032   0000149   JONES, ANGELA           75,175.71  05/01/2005  SEVENTY FIVE THOUSAND ONE HUNDRED SEVENTY FIVE DOLLARS AND 71
  000033   0000150   SMITH, ARPHIE           10,023.42  05/01/2005  TEN THOUSAND TWENTY THREE DOLLARS AND 42 CENTS
  000034   0000152   SMITH,ANNETTE RENEE      1,002.34  05/01/2005  ONE THOUSAND TWO DOLLARS AND 34 CENTS
                                                                                                                  More...
 F3=Exit    F12=Cancel   F19=Left   F20=Right   F21=Split
```

Figure 5.4: This is the output that the Query Manager query generated.

If we created a Query Manager report form to match this data, the output shown in Figure 5.5 could be generated, resulting in a printable check form from a simple Query Manager report.

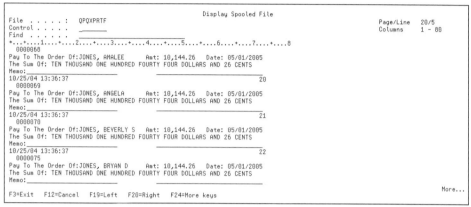

Figure 5.5: This output represents a printable check format.

As you can see, the TextDollars function gives us the ability to extend the capabilities of the Query Manager application.

As I mentioned, it's also possible to use a table function within Query Manager. Figure 5.6 shows an example of a Query Manager query that uses the WeekEndDates table function.

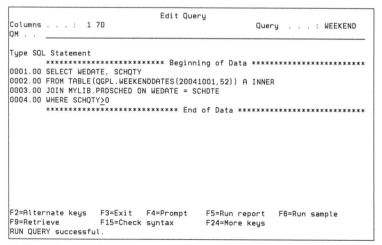

Figure 5.6: This Query Manager query uses the WeekEndDates table function.

In this example, we use the table function as the primary table for our query. An inner join expression is used to also select records from a scheduled production table based on matching the WEDATE value to the value of the scheduled date field (SCHDTE). The scheduled quantity (SCHQTY) field is also selected within our query. When this statement is executed, a row will be returned for each record in the table PRDSCHED, which has a record for the field SCHDTE with a matching value for the field WEDATE from our table function. Figure 5.7 shows a sample of the output that this Query Manager query would generate.

```
                                  Display Report
Query . . . . .:    QGPL.WEEKEND                Width . . .:        71
Form  . . . . .:    *SYSDFT                      Column  . .:         1
Control   . . . .   _____
Line    ....+....1....+....2....+....3....+....4....+....5....+....6....+....7.
.                 WEDATE          SCHQTY
                ------------    --------------
000029     20,050,430            201
000030     20,050,507             47
000031     20,050,514             94
000032     20,050,521            141
000033     20,050,528            188
000034     20,050,604             26
000035     20,050,611             73
000036     20,050,618            120
000037     20,050,625            168
000038     20,050,702             13
000039     20,050,709             60
000040     20,050,716            107
000041     20,050,723            154
000042     20,050,730            201
                                                              More...
 F3=Exit     F12=Cancel    F19=Left    F20=Right    F21=Split
This is a sample report.  Data is incomplete.
```

Figure 5.7: This output is generated using an SQL table function.

As you can see, the output from our table function is treated as any other table would be. We are even able to use the value of the WEDATE field as part of the join expression.

These examples help to illustrate the powerful functionality that can be added to Query Manager reports by using user-defined scalar and table functions.

Embedded SQL

Perhaps one of the most powerful features of the iSeries implementation of SQL is the ability to incorporate segments of SQL code within a host language. The iSeries supports embedded SQL statements within programs written in RPG, ILE RPG, COBOL, PL/I, C/C++, and REXX. The one common (or somewhat common) element among each of these languages is how SQL statements are executed. Each group of SQL statements begins with one form or another of the command EXEC SQL, which takes on different forms in different languages. Table 5.1 shows examples of an embedded SQL statement coded into each of these host languages.

Table 5.1: Examples of Embedded SQL Statements in Various Languages

Language	Embedded SQL Sample
RPG	C/EXEC SQL UPDATE PAYROLL C+ SET RATE = RATE 1.06 C+ WHERE EMPNO = :SELEMP C/END-EXEC
ILE RPG	C/EXEC SQL UPDATE PAYROLL C+ SET RATE = RATE 1.06 C+ WHERE EMPNO = :SELEMP C/END-EXEC

COBOL	EXEC SQL
	    UPDATE PAYROLL
	    SET RATE = RATE * 1.06
	    WHERE EMPNO = :SELEMP
	 END-EXEC.

PL/I	EXEC SQL
	    UPDATE PAYROLL
	    SET RATE = RATE * 1.06
	    WHERE EMPNO = :SELEMP;

C/C++	EXEC SQL
	    UPDATE PAYROLL
	    SET RATE = RATE * 1.06
	    WHERE EMPNO = :SELEMP;

REXX	EXECSQL "UPDATE PAYROLL SET RATE = RATE * 1.06 WHERE EMPNO = :SELEMP"

You'll note that RPG, ILE RPG, and COBOL all require the END-EXEC statement to identify the end of an embedded SQL group. Within RPG and ILE RPG,

EXEC SQL and END-EXEC are specified as compiler directives. PL/I and C/C++ both simply use the EXEC SQL command to begin the SQL segment and a semicolon to end the SQL segment. REXX uses the EXECSQL command, which contains the SQL statement embedded in quotes.

While the examples in the table perform an update operation, it's actually possible to execute a range of SQL statements within a host language. For example, we can use a SELECT statement in place of file specifications in an RPG or ILE RPG program. It's even possible to create an ILE RPG program with no F-specs that reads and writes data through the use of embedded SQL statements. The ILE RPG program shown in Figure 5.7 is an example of a simple program that reads data from a single file.

```
 *
 *   Program: SMP001RG
 *
 *   Description: Sample ILE RPG Program
 *
 *   Compile command: CRTBNDRPG PGM(mylib/SMP001RG)
 *                              SRCFILE(mylib/QRPGLESRC)
 *                              SRCRBR(SMP001RG)
 *
FORDERS      IF   E            K DISK
FPRINTOUT    O    E              PRINTER
 *
C                      READ        ORDERS
 *
C                      DOU         %EOF(ORDERS)
C                      WRITE       PRT1
C                      READ        ORDERS
C                      ENDDO
 *
C                      EVAL        *INLR = *ON
C                      RETURN
```

Figure 5.8: This simple ILE RPG program reads a physical file.

As you can see, this simple example reads data from the file ORDERS and writes data out to the printer file PRINTOUT. This program uses a technique you're probably already familiar with to perform this task.

The code shown in Figure 5.9 contains a new version of this program that replaces the file specs and file operations with embedded SQL statements.

```
*
*   Program: SMP002RG
*
*   Description: Sample SQL-ILE RPG Program
*
*   Compile command: CRTSQLRPGI PGM(mylib/SMP002RG)
*                               SRCFILE(mylib/QRPGLESRC) COMMIT(*NONE)
*                               SRCRBR(SMP002RG) OBJTYPE(*PGM)
*
FPRINTOUT  O    E              PRINTER
*
DORDRS          E DS                    EXTNAME(ORDERS)
*
C/EXEC SQL
C+ DECLARE ORD_CSR1 CURSOR FOR SELECT * FROM ORDERS
C/END-EXEC
C/EXEC SQL
C+ OPEN ORD_CSR1
C/END-EXEC
C/EXEC SQL
C+ FETCH NEXT FROM ORD_CSR1 Into :ORDRS
C/END-EXEC
C                   DOW       SQLCOD <> 100 and SQLCOD >= 0
C                   WRITE     PRT1
C/EXEC SQL
C+ FETCH NEXT FROM ORD_CSR1 Into :ORDRS
C/END-EXEC
C                   ENDDO
*
C                   EVAL      *iNLR = *ON
C/EXEC SQL
C+ CLOSE ORD_CSR1
C/END-EXEC
C                   RETURN
```

Figure 5.9: This is the same program as in Figure 5.8, but it uses embedded SQL.

In this example, the file spec is replaced by the DECLARE CURSOR statement. DECLARE CURSOR defines a source table without actually opening the file itself. The OPEN statement takes care of opening the file. This means that we can redefine the cursor based on different host variables by closing and reopening the cursor. The READ operation code is replaced by the FETCH NEXT operation. The %EOF conditioning is replaced by using the value returned in SQLCOD. In the example above, an SQLCOD value of 100 indicates a record-not-found condition. Note that we need to create an external data structure based on our original file to allow the FETCH statement to pass the values for our file into the program.

The real beauty of using embedded SQL is that you can select only the fields you need and then create complex SELECT statements containing data from multiple files. It's also possible to use a SELECT statement to retrieve a single value in place of a CHAIN operation. For example, the following CHAIN operation obtains an item description by retrieving a record from the file ITEMS.

```
C       ITEMNO      CHAIN     ITEMS
C                   IF        %FOUND(ITEMS)
C                   EVAL      DESC = ITDESC
C                   ENDIF
```

This example can be replaced using an embedded SQL statement as shown here:

```
C/EXEC SQL
C+ SELECT ITDESC INTO :DESC FROM ORDERS WHERE ITRMNO = :ITEMS
C/END-EXEC
```

This statement retrieves the value of the field ITDESC from the table ITEMS into the field DESC.

In each of these examples, you'll notice that variables are passed between the embedded SQL and the host language by preceding the variable name with a colon (:).

The ability to use SQL statements such as this to retrieve data is greatly enhanced by the use of user-defined scalar and table functions. The example shown in Figure 5.10 uses the TEXTDATE scalar function we created in chapter 4 as part of a complex cursor within an ILE RPG application.

```
... RPG code
    C/EXEC SQL
    C+ DECLARE       INV_CSR1 CURSOR FOR SELECT INVNO, INVUST, CUSNAM,
    C+               INAMT, INQTY QGPL.TEXTDATE(INVDAT) FROM INVOICES
    C+               INNER JOIN CUSTOMERS ON INCUST = CUSTNO
    C/END-EXEC
    C/EXEC SQL
    C+ OPEN INV_CSR1
    C/END-EXEC
    C/EXEC SQL
    C+ FETCH NEXT FROM INV_CSR1 INTO :INVN, :CUST, :CNAM,
    C+             :INVA, :IQTY, :INDATE
    C/END-EXEC
    C                DOW       SQLCOD <> 100 and SQLCOD >= 0
    C                WRITE     INVOICE
    C/EXEC SQL
    C+ FETCH NEXT FROM INV_CSR1 INTO :INVN, :CUST, :CNAM,
    C+             :INVA, :IQTY, :INDATE
    C/END-EXEC
    C                ENDDO
... RPG code
```

Figure 5.10: This embedded SQL code uses a user-defined scalar function.

This example retrieves records from the table INVOICES. The TEXTDATE function allows us to covert the value of the INVDAT field into a long text date format. This example also illustrates using a joined SELECT statement. In this example, we are able to retrieve a customer name value from the table CUSTOMERS for each record in the table INVOICES. This simplifies the process you might otherwise use to retrieve this data whereby you would read the record from the INVOICES table and then perform a CHAIN operation to the CUSTOMERS table to retrieve the CUSNAM value.

It's also possible to perform file updates using embedded SQL. Figure 5.11 contains a somewhat modified version of the example in Figure 5.10, which performs a file update.

```
... RPG code
    C/EXEC SQL
    C+ DECLARE INV_CSR1 CURSOR FOR SELECT INVNO, INVUST, CUSNAM,
    C+          INAMT, INQTY QGPL.TEXTDATE(INVDAT) FROM INVOICES
    C+          INNER JOIN CUSTOMERS ON INCUST = CUSTNO
    C+          FOR UPDATE OF PRTFLG
    C/END-EXEC
    C/EXEC SQL
    C+ OPEN INV_CSR1
    C/END-EXEC
    C/EXEC SQL
    C+ FETCH NEXT FROM INV_CSR1 INTO :INVN, :CUST, :CNAM,
    C+             :INVA, :IQTY, :INDATE
    C/END-EXEC
    C                   DOW        SQLCOD <> 100 and SQLCOD >= 0
    C                   WRITE      INVOICE
    C/EXEC SQL
    C+ UPDATE CURRENT OF INV_CSR1 SET PRTFLG = 'P'
    C/END-EXEC
    C/EXEC SQL
    C+ FETCH NEXT FROM INV_CSR1 INTO :INVN, :CUST, :CNAM,
    C+             :INVA, :IQTY, :INDATE
    C/END-EXEC
    C                   ENDDO
... RPG code
```

Figure 5.11: This version of our example performs an UPDATE operation.

As this example illustrates, the addition of the UPDATE CURRENT OF statement allows us to update the current record from the specified SQL cursor with the value or values provided. This technique is somewhat more secure than using the UPDATE operation code in ILE RPG because it allows us to identify the specific field or fields to be updated, thereby ensuring that a field that may have unintentionally had its value changed does not get updated when the data is written out. This technique offers similar functionality to that available using the %FIELDS function in RPG.

It's also possible to perform INSERT, UPDATE, and DELETE operations based on a global criteria rather than just the current record. The code segment in Figure 5.12 is an example.

```
C                       IF        *INKD
C/EXEC SQL
C+ DELETE FROM ORDERS WHERE PURGFL = 'Y'
C/END-EXEC
C                       ENDIF
```

Figure 5.12: Here's an example of executing an embedded SQL DELETE statement.

In this example, when a user presses the F4 key, the DELETE statement will be executed, resulting in all records with the PURGFL field equal to 'Y' being deleted. This type of example allows us to replace what would otherwise be a much more complex program with a single line of SQL code.

As I mentioned earlier, it's also possible to use a user-defined table function within embedded SQL. Figure 5.13 shows an example of using the user-defined table function GetFields that we examined in chapter 4.

```
      C/EXEC SQL
      C+ DECLARE CSR1 CURSOR FOR SELECT FILE, FIELD
      C+           FROM TABLE(MYLIB.GETFIELDS(:TABLENAME, :LIBNAME)
      C/END-EXEC
...
      C/EXEC SQL
      C+ OPEN CSR1
      C/END-EXEC
      C/EXEC SQL
      C+ FETCH NEXT FROM CSR1 INTO :FILNAM, :FLDNAM
      C/END-EXEC
      C                     DOW       SQLCOD <> 100 and SQLCOD >= 0
      C                     WRITE     SFLFLD
      C/EXEC SQL
      C+ FETCH NEXT FROM CSR1 INTO :FILNAM, :FLDNAM
      C/END-EXEC
      C                     ENDDO
...
```

Figure 5.13: This sample uses a table function within embedded SQL.

This example writes the values of the fields FILNAM and FLDNAM out to the sub-file record SFLFLD. In this sample, the values for each of the table function's parameters are supplied using host variables. This allows a user to key these values into an entry field and write out a subfile display containing each of the field names.

We can also call stored procedures from within embedded SQL. The sample code shown in Figure 5.14 calls an SQL stored procedure we created in chapter 3 from within an RPG program.

```
*_____
*
* Program: SQL001LE Function: Example of calling a stored proceure
*                             from within an ILE RPG program using
*                             embedded SQL statements.
*
* Create Command  CRTSQLRPGI PGM(lib/SQL001LE)
*                            SRCFILE(lib/QRPGLESRC)
*                            SRCMBR(SQL001LE)
*_____
FSQL001FM  CF   E                WORKSTN
C                     EXFMT      SQL001F1
C                     IF         *INKC=*OFF
C/EXEC SQL
C+ CALL QGPL.BLDSUMFILE(:WSITEM, :WSCUST)
C/END-EXEC
C       'File created'DSPLY
C                     EndIf
C                     Eval       *INLR=*ON
C                     Return
```

Figure 5.14: This RPG program calls an SQL stored procedure.

While each of these examples is performed with SQL embedded within an ILE RPG application, the concept would be the same within other host languages.

Now that we've examined alternatives for accessing SQL functions from within the iSeries, let's take a look at client/server options for calling functions and stored procedures.

ADO/ODBC

Windows client/server applications written in any of the popular Windows development platforms can make use of data access functionality through ActiveX Data Objects (ADO). An ADO object connects to a database through an OLE DB or an ODBC database connection. The data within these databases is accessed through the iSeries SQL engine. This means that any of the added func-tionality we build through user-defined functions and stored procedures can be accessed via ADO.

This goes back to a point I made earlier about the portability of user-defined functions and stored procedures. We've already seen how we can access these objects by embedding SQL statements into host languages. Any functions or procedures built for use on the iSeries can also be called remotely from an ADO client application. A number of options are available for development environments that support ADO. We'll take a look at using a few of these options with some of the user-defined functions and procedures we've already created.

But before we examine any specific options for development languages, I'd like to explain the components of an ADO connection. Figure 5.15 shows the ADO object model.

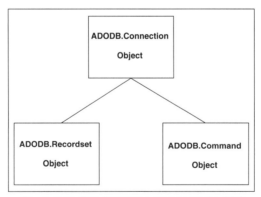

Figure 5.15: This illustration represents the ADO object model.

As this object model shows, accessing data via ADO requires that we first define an ADO connection object. This object defines the machine and database from which the data is to be retrieved, as well as the credentials used to connect to that data source. The key to the CONNECTION object is the ConnectionString property, which defines the general information described above. The following is a sample ConnectionString property.

```
objConn.ConnectionString = "DRIVER=Client Access ODBC Driver
                            (32-bit);" & _
                           "UID=user; PWD=secret; System=192.168.1.3;"
```

This example creates an ODBC connection to a data source using the Client Access ODBC driver. The UID and PWD parameters identify the user name and password used to access the iSeries server identified by the IP address shown on the system parameter. It's also possible to define a ConnectionString that uses the IBM OLE DB provider in place of the ODBC drive. This is illustrated in the following example.

```
objConn.ConnectionString = "Provider=IBMDA400; Data
                            Source=192.168.1.3; " & _
                           "User ID=user; Password=secret;"
```

In this example, the Provider value identifies that the IBMDA400 provider should be used. The Data Source value identifies the system name or IP address of the iSeries. And the User ID and Password parameters are used to provide the security credentials to log into the iSeries. A RECORDSET object is the means by which you access the actual data. The RECORDSET is defined using an SQL SELECT statement. We are able to use SELECT statements with complex join definitions to bring together data from multiple tables as part of our data set. The example below uses the CONNECTIONSTRING object defined in the previous example.

```
objRs.Open "SELECT * FROM QSYS2.SYSTABLES", objConn
```

This example retrieves records from the SYSTABLES system view. The second parameter identifies a previously defined ADO connection object. An ADO COMMAND object is primarily used to execute a stored procedure on the server. The example below calls a stored procedure named MYPROC.

```
objCmd.ActiveConnection = objConn
objCmd.Execute "CALL MYLIB.MYPROC(1,2,3)"
```

This example first associates the CONNECTION object with our COMMAND object using the ActiveConnection method. Then, the Execute method calls the stored procedure. COMMAND objects can also be used from a client application to execute action-based SQL statements (INSERT, DELETE, UPDATE).

ADO from Excel

As I mentioned earlier, there are many options for accessing ADO data from a Windows client. The first option I'd like to explore is using these objects from within an Excel spreadsheet. To use ADO from within Excel, we're actually going to build some VBScript macros into a spreadsheet. Start by opening Excel and selecting Macros from the Tools menu. Then, select Visual Basic Editor, as shown in Figure 5.16.

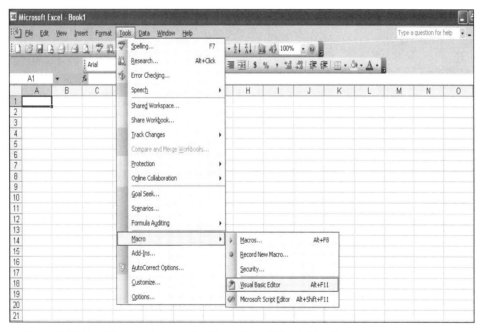

Figure 5.16: Use this menu to open the Visual Basic Editor in Excel.

The Visual Basic Editor within Excel is an editor that is actually common to all Microsoft Office components. It's a somewhat smaller version of the editor you would use in Microsoft Visual Studio. The VBScript language includes a subset of the Visual Basic language but also includes some added functionality specifically related to the Office applications themselves. This VBScript code we'll be creating sits inside and "behind" the Excel spreadsheet and is able to interact with the spreadsheet itself. Figure 5.17 shows the workbench that is displayed.

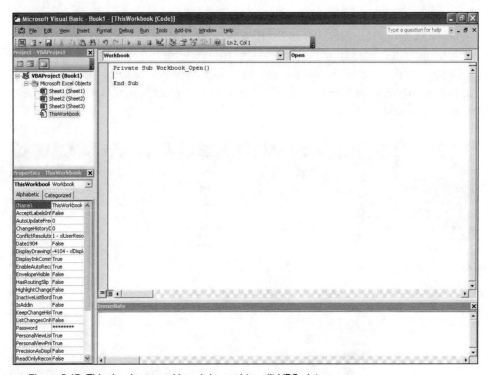

Figure 5.17: This developer workbench is used to edit VBScripts.

To create this example, return to the Excel window and display the Visual Basic toolbar by selecting View > Toolbars > Visual Basic. When the Visual Basic toolbar is displayed, select the Control Toolbox icon. Now, find the Command Button icon to insert a new Command button into Sheet1. Use the example shown in Figure 5.18 to format the Command button as well as the first four columns in the first row.

Now, right-click the new Command button and select Properties. From within the Properties dialog, change the Caption property to Load, and change the

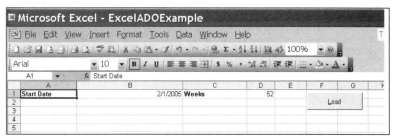

Figure 5.18: Use this example to format the spreadsheet.

Name property to LoadFields. Close the Properties dialog and select View Code. The design workbench will refresh, and the Click event for our Command button will be displayed.

Before we can create our code, we need to make this project aware that it needs to use ADO. Do this by selecting Tools > References. Search through the list for the newest version of Microsoft ActiveX Data Objects from the window shown in Figure 5.19.

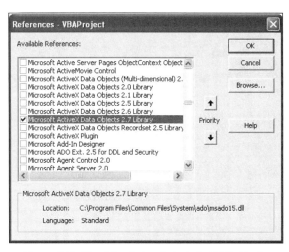

Figure 5.19: Use this window to include ADO objects.

Once we've created a reference to the ADO object library, we're ready to create our code. Within the LoadFields.Click subroutine, insert the code shown in Figure 5.20.

```
Private Sub LoadFields_Click()
Dim objConn As New ADODB.Connection, objRs As New ADODB.Recordset
Dim lngStrDate As Long, intWeeks As Integer, X As Long, Y As Long

lngStrDate = (Year(Sheet1.Cells(1, 2))*10000)+(Month(Sheet1.Cells(1, 2))*100) _
             + Day(Sheet1.Cells(1, 2))
intWeeks = Sheet1.Cells(1, 4)
Sheet1.Range("A3", "A65535").ClearContents

objConn.ConnectionString = "DRIVER=Client Access ODBC Driver (32-bit);" & _
                           "REMARKS = 1;LIBVIEW = 1; LanguageID = ENU;" & _
                           "PKG=QGPL/DEFAULT(IBM),2,0,1,0,512;" & _
                           "DFTPKGLIB =QGPL; SYSTEM=192.168.1.3"
objConn.Open

objRs.Open "SELECT QGPL.TEXTDATE(DECIMAL(DIGITS(WEMONTH) || DIGITS(WEDAY)" & _
           "|| DIGITS(WEYEAR),8,0)) FROM TABLE(DEVFAUSTM.WEEKENDDATES(" & _
           lngStrDate & "," & intWeeks & ")) AS DATES", objConn
If objRs.EOF Then
    MsgBox "Error Occurred", vbOKOnly
Else

If objConn.Errors.Count > 0 Then
    msg = ""
    For X = 0 To objConn.Errors.Count - 1
      msg = msg & objConn.Errors(X).Description
    Next
    MsgBox msg, vbOKOnly
Else
Sheet1.Cells(3, 1) = "Week Ending Date"

Y = 3

Do Until objRs.EOF
Y = Y + 1
Sheet1.Cells(Y, 1) = "'" & objRs.Fields(0).Value

objRs.MoveNext
Loop
Sheet1.Cells(Y + 2, 1) = "* Load Complete"

End If
End If

objRs.Close
objConn.Close
End Sub
```

Figure 5.20: This code retrieves data from the iSeries.

This example begins by defining the ADODB.Connection and ADODB.Recordset objects. Next, we declare variables to read data from the two spreadsheet cells containing the parameters for our table function. This example makes use of the WeekEndDates table function and passes these two variables as parameters to that function. Then, this code clears the portion of the spreadsheet that will contain the data. After that, we define the ConnectionString property for our CONNECTION object. Once the connection is opened, we're ready to retrieve the data using the WeekEndDates function. This example also uses the TextDate function to convert the resulting weekend date value to a string representation of the date.

After the data source is opened, some error handling is done so that if no records are returned or if an error occurs in the connection, a message is displayed to the user. Otherwise, the application reads through all of the records in our table and populates the value from the first field in our recordset into a corresponding cell on the spreadsheet. (Note that you'll need to replace the value for the SYSTEM, shown above as 192.168.1.3, with the name or IP address of your iSeries.) We complete this process by closing the recordset and connection objects.

After you've entered this code into the event module, save your spreadsheet and close the workbench. When your spreadsheet is redisplayed, click the Exit Design Mode icon on the Visual Basic toolbar to activate your Command button. Now, key in a start date and the number of weeks in the corresponding cell and click the Load button. The values for the specified dates will be populated into your spreadsheet automatically. Figure 5.21 shows a sample of the results that will be displayed.

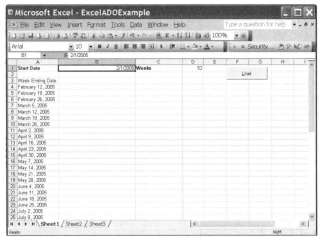

Figure 5.21: Here are the results of using ADO within an Excel spreadsheet.

This example helps to illustrate the portability of both user-defined scalar and table functions. We're able to use the same functions we used embedded in an RPG program to retrieve data into an Excel worksheet.

Active Server Pages and ADO

In addition to Microsoft Excel, it's also possible to use ADO from within an Active Server Pages (ASP) application. ASPs can be used to create dynamic Web pages using VBScript source as the development language. To use an ASP, you will need a Windows server with Microsoft Internet Information Server (IIS). There are alternatives to this setup that allow you to host ASP applications on other platforms and Web servers, but IIS is the most common platform for ASP deployment. The example we'll explore assumes that you have an existing IIS server that can host the ASP sample application.

As I described earlier, ADO also has the ability to execute a stored procedure on the iSeries. The CrossTab stored procedure we created in chapter 3 is an unusual stored procedure in that it actually acts more like a table function. Figure 5.22 contains the source for an ASP that calls the CrossTab procedure.

```
<HTML>
<BODY>
<%
Set objConn = Server.CreateObject("ADODB.Connection")
Set objRs = Server.CreateObject("ADODB.Recordset")
Set objCmd = Server.CreateObject("ADODB.Command")

objConn.ConnectionTimeout = 999
objConn.CommandTimeout = 999
objConn.Open "DRIVER=Client Access ODBC Driver (32-bit); " & _
             "REMARKS = 1;LIBVIEW = 1; LanguageID = ENU; " & _
             " PKG=QGPL/DEFAULT(IBM),2,0,1,0,512; " & _
             " UID = user; PWD = secret;" & _
             "DFTPKGLIB = QGPL; SYSTEM=192.168.1.3"

stmt = "{CALL CrossTab('QSYS2.SYSTABLES', " & _
       " 'TABLE_OWNER','TABLE_SCHEMA','ROW_LENGTH')}"
```

Figure 5.22: This Active Server Page uses ADO with the iSeries (part 1 of 2).

```
objRs.Open stmt, objConn
Response.Write "<TABLE BORDER = 1><TR>"
For x = 0 To objRs.Fields.Count - 1
Response.Write "<TH>" & objRs.Fields(x).Name & "</TH>"
Next
Response.Write "</TR>"
Do Until objRs.EOF
Response.Write "<TR>"
For x = 0 To objRs.Fields.Count - 1
Response.Write "<TD>" & objRs.Fields(x).Value & "</TD>"
Next
Response.Write "</TR>"
objRs.MoveNext
Loop
Response.Write "</TABLE>"
objRs.Close
objConn.Close
%>
</BODY>
</HTML>
```

Figure 5.22: This Active Server Page uses ADO with the iSeries (part 2 of 2).

As you can see in this example, an ASP combines HTML with VBScript code to create dynamic output. As with the Excel example, our ASP starts by defining the ADO Connection and ADO Recordset objects. Note that we have to use a different method to create these objects from an ASP. The Server.CreateObject method identifies that the object is created at the Web server. Remember that an ASP runs on a Web server but is displayed on a Web browser client. We also open the connection using a slightly different method than we used in the Excel example. Using this method, the objConn.Open method is followed by the ConnectionString. This saves an additional step of first defining the ConnectionString. Also note that the UID and PWD parameters are included to pass the user name and password. From the Excel example, if the user is not currently connected to the iSeries, a user ID and password prompt is displayed. Since an ASP runs on the server, the prompting can't occur on the client. In this example, the SQL statement used to initiate the stored procedure is placed in the string variable "stmt." This example retrieves data from the SYSTABLES system view and generates a summary crosstab of this information, which is then displayed as an HTML table. Figure 5.23 shows the output from this example.

TABLE_SCHEMA	AGEVANTE	ANONFTP	CUSTSVC	LBELL	MFAUST	OFFICE	OPERATOR	PKMS1	QCOLSRV	QDFT(
QSYS2	0	0	0	0	0	0	0	0	0	0
QSQL	0	0	0	0	0	0	0	0	0	0
QMPGDATA	0	0	0	0	0	0	0	0	14460	0
QDEVTOOLS	0	0	0	0	0	0	0	0	0	0
QSSP	0	0	0	0	0	0	0	0	0	0
QMU400	0	0	0	0	0	0	0	0	0	0
QDSNX	0	0	0	0	0	0	0	0	0	0
QEYINS97	0	0	0	0	0	0	0	0	0	0
QUMEDIA	0	0	0	0	0	0	0	0	0	0
QADM	0	0	0	0	0	0	0	0	0	0
QPEXDATA	0	0	0	0	0	0	0	0	0	0
QSR	0	0	0	0	0	0	0	0	0	0
QDNS	0	0	0	0	0	0	0	0	0	0
QPDA	0	0	0	0	0	0	0	0	0	0
QPFRDATA	0	0	0	0	0	0	0	0	0	0
QIWS	0	0	0	0	0	0	0	0	0	0
QSPL	0	0	0	0	0	0	0	0	0	0

Figure 5.23: This is the output generated by our ASP.

Remember that the values returned by the CrossTab procedure emulate results returned by an SQL SELECT. An SQL SELECT statement that defines the fields to be returned could easily replace the value defined on the variable "stmt" in Figure 5.22. This example helps us to accentuate the universal appeal of user-defined functions and procedures. Because SQL is the backbone of so many data retrieval tools on the iSeries, user-defined functions and stored procedures take on a much wider range of possible uses. The same stored procedure we used in this ASP example could be used from within an RPG program or even be called from a Java applet.

JDBC

The Java programming language has become one of the most widely used application development languages on the market. One of its most attractive features is its portability. The primary method for achieving data access from within a Java applet is via the Java Database Connectivity (JDBC) classes. As with ADO, JDBC connectivity is a multi-step process. Figure 5.24 contains the source for our Java applet.

```
import java.io.*;
import java.sql.*;
import java.util.*;
import java.awt.*;
    public class MilesCSV extends Frame {
        public static void main(java.lang.String[] args) {

        String output = args[0];
        final int EXIT_ERROR = 1;
try {
Class.forName("com.ibm.db2.jdbc.app.DB2Driver");
}
catch (ClassNotFoundException cnfe) {
System.err.println("ClassNotFoundException for " + cnfe.getMessage());
cnfe.printStackTrace();
System.exit(EXIT_ERROR);
}
try {
FileOutputStream out = new FileOutputStream(output);
PrintStream p = new PrintStream( out );
Properties pr = new Properties();
      pr.put("user", "user");
      pr.put("password", "secret");
String constr = "jdbc:db2:*local;translate binary=true";
Connection con = DriverManager.getConnection(constr, pr);
Statement statement = con.createStatement();
String sqlStmt = "SELECT SHPZIP, WHSZIP, QGPL.GETMILES(SHPZIP, WHSZIP, 'M')
";

sqlStmt = sqlStmt + "AS DIST FROM MYLIB.ORDERS";
ResultSet rs = statement.executeQuery(sqlStmt);
ResultSetMetaData rsd = rs.getMetaData();
String rec = "";
for (int i=1; i<=rsd.getColumnCount(); i++) {
rec = rec + rsd.getColumnName(i);
if (i < rsd.getColumnCount()) {
rec = rec + ", ";
}
}
p.println(rec);
while (rs.next()) {
rec = "";
for (int i=1; i<=rsd.getColumnCount(); i++) {
rec = rec + "\"" + rs.getString(i) + "\"";
if (i < rsd.getColumnCount()) {
rec = rec + ", ";
}
}
```

Figure 5.24: This Java example uses the SQL GETMILES function (part 1 of 2).

143

```
p.println(rec);
}
p.close();
rs.close();
}
catch (SQLException sqle) {
System.err.println("An SQL exception occurred:");
do {
System.err.println("Message:    " + sqle.getMessage());
System.err.println("SQLState:   " + sqle.getSQLState());
System.err.println("ErrorCode: " + sqle.getErrorCode());
} while (sqle.getNextException() != null);
}
catch (FileNotFoundException fnfe) {
System.err.println("File Not Found Exception");
}
}
}
```

Figure 5.24: This Java example uses the SQL GETMILES function (part 2 of 2).

This example uses the com.ibm.db2.jdbc.app.DB2Driver JDBC driver to access the iSeries database. The code reads data from a table containing shipment information including a "ship-to" ZIP code (SHPZIP) and a warehouse ZIP code (WHSZIP) as well as the distance between the two ZIP codes, which is calculated using the GetMiles scalar function. The data read is written to a comma-delimited text file. After the connection to the database is made, the application creates the file to contain the comma-separated values (CSV) data. The Statement command is used to create a new object, which in turn is used to create the ResultSet object using the executeQuery command. A Java result set acts much like an ADO Recordset object. FileOutputStream creates the CSV file specified on the single argument supported by this applet. In addition to the ResultSet object "rs," we also have a ResultSetMetaData object named "rsd." These two objects contain the information that would be found in the ADO Recordset object. While "rs" contains the actual data set data, "rsd" contains information about the data set, such as record counts. The values read from each of the columns in the result set are separated with comma characters (,) and concatenated into a single string for each row in the result set, which is written out to the FileOuputStream.

To build this example, enter the Qshell utility using the iSeries QSH command. Assuming you've stored this source in your home directory (in my case, /home/MFAUST), navigate to that folder or whatever folder contains the source using the change directory (cd) command. This file will be named MilesCSV.java. Now, compile the Java source into an executable "class" file using the javac command shown in Figure 5.25.

```
                        QSH Command Entry

    $
  > cd '/home/FAUSTM'
    $
  > javac MilesCSV.java
    $




  ===>   _____


 F3=Exit    F6=Print  F9=Retrieve F12=Disconnect
  F13=Clear F17=Top   F18=Bottom   F21=CL command entry
```

Figure 5.25: Compile the Java MilesCSV.java program.

Once this compile completes, verify that the class file was created using the "ls" command. You should see the file MilesCSV.class. You can execute your new Java applet from the Qshell command line using the command below.

```
Java MilesCSV.class "/home/FAUSTM/mycsvfile.csv"
```

This example requires that you have a table named ORDERS in library MYLIB with fields SHPZIP and WHSZIP, which represent five-digit numeric ZIP codes. The argument shown in quotes represents the target location and file name for the output file. Once you've successfully executed this statement, you will find the comma-delimited output file in the specified folder. Figure 5.26 shows a sample of the CSV file output by this command.

```
SHPZIP, WHSZIP, DIST
"18062", "27804", "336.804744"
"18062", "06037", "164.301566"
"18062", "76180", "1305.908250"
"18062", "33441", "1014.741149"
"18062", "74120", "1142.982091"
"18062", "33458", "973.652774"
"18062", "33311", "1027.275577"
"18062", "32807", "888.177349"
"18062", "34691", "943.883482"
"18062", "33647", "938.353299"
"18062", "32073", "794.355565"
"18062", "32714", "882.763075"
"18062", "33434", "1010.922009"
"18062", "48076", "419.015556"
"18062", "33781", "964.955550"
"18062", "32953", "886.096958"
"18062", "43017", "399.004597"
```

Figure 5.26: This is the output from MilesCSV.java.

Make the Most of Stored Procedures and Functions

These examples helps to reinforce the real universal appeal of stored procedures and functions. They allow you to reuse building blocks from one application to another and even share them between development environments and platforms. Therefore, you can make better and more efficient use of your application development resources by building pieces of code that can be reused over and over again.

I hope this book has set you on the path to making the most of SQL functions and stored procedures.

Example Installation Instructions

This book includes a variety of application examples in a range of programming languages, including SQL, RPG, and VBScript, just to name a few. To download the files, go to the MC Press Web site at www.mcpressonline.com and select Site Help > MC-Store.com > MC Product Support > Product Updates. Then select this book's title.

In this appendix, I'll explain how to create these examples for use with your iSeries. Included with the companion code for each chapter of this book, you will find a text document that has details on each example.

Let me start by explaining the naming convention used for each of the files contained within the companion code. The table below shows the file suffixes used along with a description of the source contained within the file.

Code File Suffixes	
File Extension	**Description**
.sql	Structured Query Language—These files contain SQL source that can be used to create user-defined stored procedures and functions.
.clp	CL program—These files must be uploaded to the iSeries in a QCLSRC source physical file and compiled using CRTCLPGM.
.rpg	ILE RPG program—These files must be uploaded to the iSeries into a QRPGLESRC source physical file prior to compilation.
.sqlrpg	ILE RPG with embedded SQL—As with ILE RPG applications, these files must be uploaded to a QRPGLESRC source physical file and compiled using the CRTSQLRPGI command.
.asp	Active Server Page document—These files must be loaded on a Web server capable of handling ASP applications.
.java	Java applet—These files must be uploaded to the iSeries into an Integrated File System (IFS) folder and compiled using the "javac" Qshell command.
.savf	iSeries Save File—These files must be uploaded to the iSeries and restored.
.vbs	VBScript language—These files can be executed from applications supporting the Visual Basic Scripting language, such as Microsoft Office.
.xls	Excel spreadsheet—These files can be read by any spreadsheet application that supports Microsoft Excel files.

SQL

The book contains many SQL examples, and you have several options for how to execute this code on the iSeries. Let's explore the options for executing SQL examples.

RUNSQLSTM

The Run SQL Statement (RUNSQLSTM) command can be used with a source physical file member that contains the required SQL statements. It is possible to upload any of the SQL sample code files into a source physical file and execute the code using this command. This process requires the following steps.

1. Create a new source physical file to contain your SQL code using the command CRTSRCPF FILE(MYLIB/QSQLSRC) RCDLEN(240). Note that I set the record length for the source physical file to 240. This allows for more code space on each line of the SQL statements.

2. Send the required source to the newly created source physical file using the iSeries Access file transfer application as shown here:

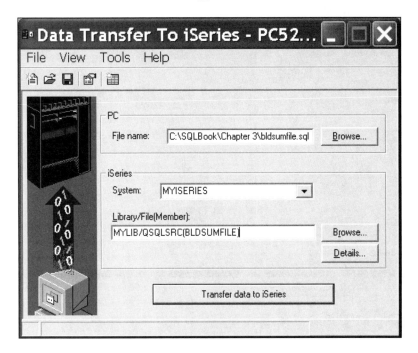

3. Once the file has been successfully uploaded, execute the code using the following RUNSQLSTM command:

```
RUNSQLSTM SRCFILE(MYLIB/QSQLSRC) SRCMBR(BLDSUMFILE)
COMMIT(*NONE) NAMING(*SQL)
```

This method allows you to keep a copy of the SQL source on your iSeries for the purposes of modifying and re-creating user-defined procedures or functions.

iSeries Navigator

As I explained earlier, the iSeries navigator tool has its own utility to execute SQL statements on the iSeries. You can access "Run SQL Scripts" by expanding the Databases group, selecting the icon representing your iSeries, expanding the Folders group, and finally selecting a library under that group. The "Run an SQL script" option will appear in the lower right of the frame as shown here:

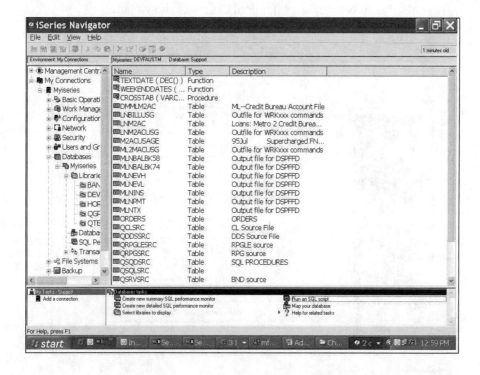

One nice thing about using iSeries Navigator is that the SQL Script tool is the default application for files with the .SQL extension. This means that since the SQL source files included are named with the extension .SQL, they will be loaded into this application by default, so double-clicking one of these files from Windows Explorer will display the window below.

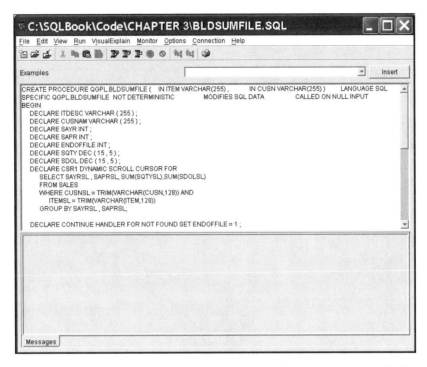

From this window, you can execute the code and receive error messages in the lower pane. You can also use the Visual Explain option to debug your code during execution.

With this method, the code is not stored in an iSeries source physical file member. However, the source for a user-defined procedure or function can be retrieved using the Generate Source option from iSeries Navigator.

CL, RPG, and SQLRPG

While each of these programming languages requires a different compiler, the general process for getting the program members onto the iSeries is the same. Your best option is to copy these files to a matching iSeries source physical file (QCLSRC for CL programs, QRPGLESRC for RPG or SQLRPG). When you create the iSeries Access transfer, it's important to make sure that you set the options for the iSeries file properly. This screen is accessed by selecting the

Details button from the main data transfer window. Set the options as shown below.

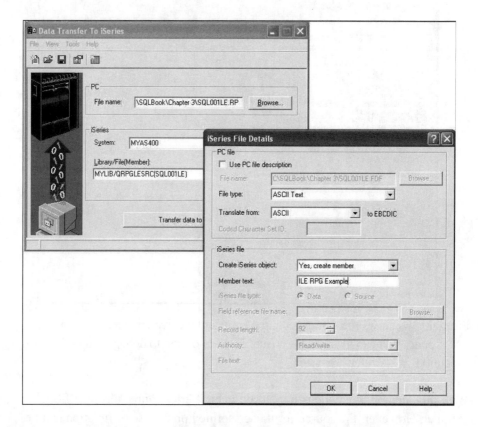

Make sure that the Create iSeries Object option is set to either "Yes, create member" if the source member doesn't already exist on your iSeries or "No, replace member only" if it does and you are re-uploading. You can also set the member text from this screen.

Once the source members have been uploaded, use one of the following commands to compile the programs.

- CRTCLPGM is used to compile CL programs.

- CRTBNDRPG is used to compile ILE RPG programs.

- CRTSQLRPGLI is used to compile an ILE RPG program with embedded SQL statements using the /EXEC SQL and /END-EXEC compiler directives.

- CRTRPGMOD and CRTSRVPGM are used together when the ILE RPG program must be compiled as a service program, as is the case with the WeekEndDates table function in chapter 4.

Active Server Pages

To load any of the ASP examples, you'll need a Web server product that supports ASP applications. The most popular choice is a Microsoft Windows server running Internet Information Server (IIS). The figure below shows the IIS admin console.

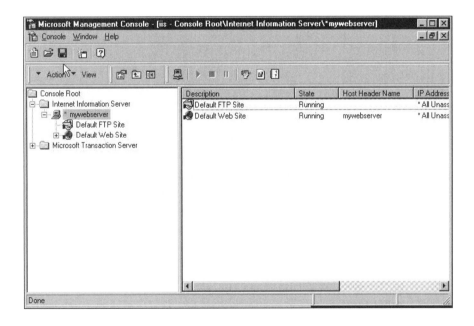

The ASP documents should be copied to the root Web folder on the Web server. You can determine this folder's location by right-clicking on the Default Web Site icon and selecting properties. The dialog below is displayed.

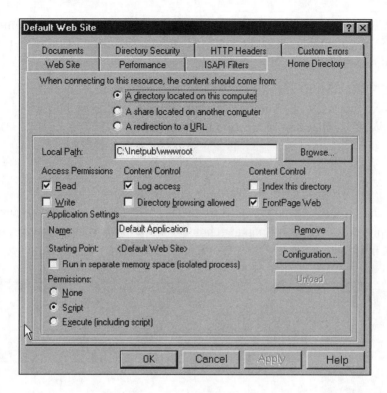

On the Home Directory tab, the Local Path box identifies the physical location on the server that contains the files for the Web site. In this case, that location is C:\Inetpub\wwwroot\. This identifies the location that needs to contain your ASP document in order for the document to be accessible from Web clients. Once the page has been placed in this folder, you can load the page from a Web browser by navigating to http://mywebserver/myaspdocument.asp, where mywebserver represents the host name or IP address of the IIS server and myaspdocument.asp represents the name of the ASP. It's also important that this server have the iSeries Access for Windows data access components (OLE DB and ODBC drivers) installed for data access purposes.

Java

The single Java example should be loaded to the iSeries through an IFS folder. You can do this by navigating to the iSeries using your iSeries Windows

Networking support, which allows you to access an iSeries IFS folder the same way you would access any other shared folder on a Windows network. This is done using a UNC path like \\MYISERIES\root\usr\. Replace MYISERIES in this UNC path with your iSeries Windows Networking name or IP address to display the Windows Explorer for the "usr" folder under the root file system on the iSeries. Once the .java file has been copied to this location, log into your iSeries and enter the Qshell environment using the QSH command. Now, navigate to the "usr" folder by typing the following command:

```
cd /usr
```

Next, you can compile the Java class from your source document:

```
javac appname.java
```

Here, appname.java is the document you copied to the "usr" folder. Once the Java class is compiled, you can execute the new Java application:

```
java appname.class
```

Here, appname.class represents the Java class you compiled in the previous step.

Save Files

The GetMiles function in chapter 4 requires an iSeries database file, which is contained in the iSeries save file zipcodes.savf. This file must be uploaded to your iSeries and restored prior to creating and executing the GetMiles function. Before you can upload this file to the iSeries, you need to create a save file to receive the data. This is done using the following command:

```
Crtsavf savf(qgpl/zipcodes)
```

Once this command has been executed, you are ready to upload the save file. But first, you need to extract it from the ZIP file containing the companion code. Extract the file to the root of the C: drive.

The best way to upload the file is by using an FTP connection. From a Windows workstation, click the Start menu, select Run, and type the command below:

```
FTP 192.168.1.3
```

Replace the IP address shown with the IP address for your iSeries. You will be prompted for your iSeries user ID and password. After entering those items, enter the commands shown below to upload the file to the iSeries.

```
bin
cd qgpl
put c:\zipcodes.savf zipcodes.zipcodes
quit
```

This series of commands first changes the transfer mode to binary. Next, the directory on the remote system is changed to QGPL library. After that, you use the "put" command to send the file into the save file created earlier. Finally, the "quit" command is issued to end the FTP connection.

Now that the file has been uploaded, go back to the iSeries and restore the file using the RSTOBJ command.

You're now ready to create the GetMiles function as described in chapter 4. It's important to note that the ZIP code data supplied with this example is based on the 2000 census and as a result may not be complete.

Additional Examples

The Microsoft Excel spreadsheet included in chapter 5 can be used with any iSeries by replacing the SYSTEM parameter within the ConnectionsString property on the objConn ADO Connection object with the valid system name or IP address for your iSeries. This identifier can be found within the LoadFields_Click() subroutine.

The other Visual Basic Script (.VBS) examples included in this book cannot be executed independently of an application that supports the VBS language. While these examples may be executed from within a Microsoft Office application, they are not designed for this purpose and are only intended as examples. As a result, there is no guarantee that these examples will execute within your environment.

Index

A
ABS, 22t, 24
Access. *See* Microsoft Access
ACOS, 22t, 24
Active Server Pages (ASP), 2, 153-154, 153, 154
    ADO/ODBC and, 140-142, 140-141, 142
ActiveX Data Objects. *See* ADO
ADO/ODBC, 18, 132-142, 156
    Active Server Pages (ASP) and, 140-142, 140-141, 142
    ADO object model in, 133, 133
    COMMAND object in, 134, 135
    CONNECTION objects in, 133, 134-135
    Java and JDBC in, 142-146, 143-144, 145, 146
    Microsoft Excel and ADO in, 135-140, 135-139
    ODBC connection creation in, 134
    RECORDSET object in, 134
    stored procedures and calls, 68
    Visual Basic and, 135-140, 135-139
ALLOW PARALLEL/DISALLOW
    PARALLEL options, user-defined functions and, 85
American National Standards Institute (ANSI), 1
AND, 44-45
ANTILOG, 22t, 24-25

arc tangent, 26
ASIN, 22t, 25
ATAN, 22t, 26
ATAN2, 22t, 26
ATANH, 22t, 26
AVG, 18t

B
BEGIN statement, 104
BIGINT, 22t, 26
BINARY, 22t
BIT_LENGTH, 22t
blank spaces, 36
BLOB, 22, 45, 46
built-in functions, 17-51

C
C/C++, embedded SQL and, 125-126, 125t
CALL statement, 57
CALLED ON NULL INPU option, user-defined functions and, 84
CALLED ON NULL INPUT option, stored procedures and, 56
CASE statement, 57-58
CEILING, 22t, 27
CHAR, 22t, 32

NOTE: Boldface numbers indicate illustrations or code listing; t indicates a table.   **159**

M

MAX, 18t, 20, 23t, 51
MICROSECOND, 22t, 39
Microsoft Access, 2
    Crosstab stored procedure for, 74-80, 74t,
        75t, 75-77, 79, 119-120, 120
MIDNIGHT_SECONDS, 22t, 40
MIN, 19t, 20, 23t
MINUTE, 22t, 39
MOD, 23t, 28
MODIFIES SQL DATA option
    stored procedures and, 56
    user-defined functions and, 84
MONMSG (Monitor Message), 97
MONTH, 22t, 38, 39
MONTHNAME, 22t
multiplication, 28
MULTIPLY_ALT, 23t, 28

N

naming conventions in SQL, 5, 147-148
NO SQL option
    stored procedures and, 56
    user-defined functions and, 84
NODENAME, 23t, 48
NOT, 45
NOW, 22t
NULL, 23t
NULLIF, 23t, 47
numeric functions, 22t, 23t, 24-29

O

OCTET_LENGTH, 22t, 22
ODBC. *See* ADO/ODBC, 132
OPEN statement, 127
OR, 44-45
ORDER BY clause, 4
    scalar functions and, 21
OUT, stored procedures and, 54

P

PARAMETER STYLE option
    stored procedures and, 55

user-defined functions and, 83
passwords, 48-49
PhnLtrToNum user-defined function, 108-109,
    108
physical files, Read Physical File (SMP001RG),
    126, 126, 127, 129
PI, 23t, 29
PL/I, embedded SQL and, 125-126, 125t
POSITION, 22t, 34
POSSTR, 22t, 34
POWER, 23t
precompilers, 1
procedures, 17, 51
    stored. *See* stored procedures
programming languages
    embedded SQL and, 125-126, 125t
    stored procedures and, 54

Q

QUARTER, 22t, 38
queries. *See* Query Manager, 121
Query Manager, 1, 120-124, 121
    built-in functions and, 17
    formatting for reports using, 121
    output of queries using, 122-123, 122, 123
    query creation for, 121-122, 122
    reports from, 121
    TextDollars (Numeric Dollar to Text Dollar
        Values) in, 122, 123
    WEDATES/WeekEndDate sample of, 120,
        123-124, 123, 124
Query/400, 120
quotation marks, 105

R

RADIANS, 23t
RAND, 23t
Read Physical File (SMP001RG), 126, 126,
    127, 129
READS SQL DATA option
    stored procedures and, 56
    user-defined functions and, 84
REAL, 23t
RECORDSET object, ADO/ODBC and, 134

NOTE: Boldface numbers indicate illustrations or code listing; t indicates a table.   **165**